THE EASY
BIG BOSS
AIR FRYER
COOKBOOK FOR
BEGINNERS

AFFORDABLE, QUICK & EASY AIR FRYER RECIPES

FOR FAST & HEALTHY MEALS

LORI PECK

INTRODUCTION

The Operation Principle of Big Boss Air Fryer

What's the secret to this appliance's magic? When you break it down, an air fryer is essentially a miniature convection oven that evenly circulates hot air around your food. Air fryers contain a fan that rapidly moves the heated air around, helping your food to crisp up without much additional oil. It also has the ability to reach very high temperatures (with some models getting up to 430F°) enhancing its ability to quickly cook foods. The device is ideal for anyone keeping a close eye on their fat consumption, as you only need a thin coat of oil on the food or on the cookware surface to prevent sticking and achieve a golden, crispy crunch. Not only does it fry, but the air fryer can also mimic other cooking functions such as baking, grilling and roasting.

Keep in mind that an air fryer is ideal for making foods in small quantities simply because the appliance does not have the physical capacity to hold a lot of food at one time. Most models can hold a from 3.5 quarts to 5.5 quarts in their fry baskets. The fry basket is the main accessory that comes with an air fryer, but some models can include other elements such as a baking pan or roasting rack. Being that the air fryer is similar to a convection oven (but way smaller), it can save you time (and electricity) over heating up your standard oven. It cooks food freakishly fast and the clean up fuss-free.

The Advantages of Big Boss Air Fryer

Air fryers have gained popularity in recent months due to the increased health awareness and more people taking deliberate action to ensure they live a healthy lifestyle. These air fryers have a lot of benefits to offer, some of which are highlighted below:

1. Cook Multiple Dishes

You can cook multiple dishes at once with an air fryer which would save you a lot of time. This is like having a skillet, a deep fryer, a toaster, and an oven together in one machine. There are also several healthy dishes you can make with it; for example, the air fryer salmon recipes. Salmon is known for its many health benefits and with an air fryer in place, you can worry less about ever having trouble cooking this fish. Other recipes you can try include the Crispy Air Fryer Baked Potatoes, Crispy Air Fryer Bacon, Air Fryer Mozzarella Sticks, Air Fryer Chocolate Chip Cookies, and Air Fryer Buttermilk Fried Chicken, among others.

2. It Helps Promote Weight Loss

Several studies have shown how fried foods can increase the risk of weight gain and obesity and other cardiovascular problems. In a study conducted in 2019 on mortality in women in the United States, it was found that "the frequent consumption of fried foods, especially fried chicken and fried fish/shellfish, was associated with a higher risk of all cause and cardiovascular mortality in women in the US".

However, you don't have to completely give up your favorite meals that require deep frying. A healthier option will be to use an air fryer for all fried meals, as it reduces your regular take of unhealthy oils, which promotes weight loss. Weight loss also reduces your risk of other health complications, including cardiovascular disease.

3. It is Safe to Use

One of the major troubles of deep frying is the risk of hot oil accidents or the consistent splashing of oil while frying. With air fryers, you can worry less about this, as there's no risk of spilling or splashing of oil. You also do not have to worry about your kids being around the kitchen. It has an auto shut feature that is activated once cooking is completed, so you don't have to worry about overheating or burnt food.

The safety standards of air fryers make them more suitable compared to the traditional deep frying method.

4. It Reduces the Risk of Toxic Acrylamide Formation

Acrylamide formation is mostly caused by high-temperature cooking such as frying, roasting, or baking. This compound is dangerous and increases the risk of various cancers, including endometrial, ovarian, pancreatic, breast, and esophageal cancers. You can however reduce this risk by using an air fryer.

The Preparations for Air-Frying Use

1. Prepare the Food You'll Be Cooking

Like in any other cooking methodology, the very first thing you should do is to prepare the food you'll be cooking. Most ingredients aren't always bite size and ready to cook, so you have to do the washing, peeling, and chopping in this step, mostly. If you're going to cook a ready-to-eat frozen product, all you'll really need to do is take it out of the freezer. Most air fryers will be able to cook it nicely straight out of the fridge, making them very convenient options for quick meals.

Those who like to make their fried dishes with batter, check with your air fryer's manufacturer whether they can work with such before doing anything. If you're going to use wet ingredients like meat and freshly washed veggies, make sure to pat them dry first as well. This way, your air fryer won't have to work extra to dry the food and get to use its capacity to actually cook your food efficiently.

You can also wrap your ingredients with aluminum foil if you want to make the most out of your cooking basket's space. This will let you cook two different dishes in one go without the need for any accessory.

2. Prepare Your Big Boss Air Fryer

Once your ingredients are prepped, the next step is to prepare your air fryer. If you're going to use accessories, grab them now. It's best to have them on hand so you can also clean them up if they need some rinsing.

You should also check if the air fryer is clean and dry before plugging it in and starting it up. Crusted old food can affect the taste and smell of your dish, so it's best to make sure that your air fryer is completely clean before using it.

3. Preheat Your Big Boss Air Fryer

While this is still a part of preparing your appliance for cooking, it's still worth a special mention because it's something a lot of people tend to forget.

To preheat, set the appliance to the highest heat level and leave it on for five minutes. That will do the trick to heat up your unit nicely in just a short amount of time.

4. Load the Ingredients into the Big Boss Air Fryer

Once the air fryer is already hot, it's ready to start cooking. Load the ingredients into its cooking basket. Make sure to use the right accessories if you intend to use them. Also, make sure to use them properly so you can make the most out of them.

5. Make Sure Not to Crowd the Cooking Basket

While loading your ingredients into the air fryer, another key trick how to use an air fryer is to avoid crowding the basket. Your ingredients will need all the space it can get so it can be exposed to hot air, while the hot air also needs room to move around.

Don't think that you'll get away with filling the basket to the brim as that will only lead to an undercooked mess.

6. Add a Bit of Oil to the Cooking Basket

The next thing you should do is to add some oil into your air fryer. While you can skip the oil entirely, it's still useful if you want to make sure that your ingredients won't stick together or to the basket while cooking. It will also give your dish the fried taste that only cooking with oil can give.

The Tips for Cleaning Big Boss Air Fryer

After your delicious meal is finished, it's time to clean your air fryer. We recommend cleaning your air fryer every time you use it, but the process of cleaning is not as daunting as you think.

➤ Unplug air fryer and take out the basket and the pan.

➤ Take a microfiber cloth and dampen it with hot water to clean the exterior of the appliance. Then, to clean the interior take a non-abrasive sponge and scrub the interior of the fryer.

➤ Next, clean the heating element by turning your air fryer upside-down and gently scrub it with a sponge.

➤ Most of the baskets and pans are dishwasher-safe, so load them into your dishwasher and let the dishwasher do the work. If you want to clean it yourself—hot water, dish soap, and a non-abrasive sponge will do the trick.

➤ If there's tough residue on your baskets and pans, soak them in hot water for about 10 minutes. Then scrub the residue away with a non-abrasive sponge.

➤ All that's left to do is to dry your appliance. We recommend to air dry the individual parts, but you can also take a cloth to dry the appliance. After it's all dry, put it back together and you'll be ready to tackle your next tasty air fryer recipe.

Bread And Breakfast

Spinach And Artichoke White Pizza

Servings: 2   Cooking Time: 18 Minutes

Ingredients:

- olive oil
- 3 cups fresh spinach
- 2 cloves garlic, minced, divided
- 1 (6- to 8-ounce) pizza dough ball*
- ½ cup grated mozzarella cheese
- ¼ cup grated Fontina cheese
- ¼ cup artichoke hearts, coarsely chopped
- 2 tablespoons grated Parmesan cheese
- ¼ teaspoon dried oregano
- salt and freshly ground black pepper

Directions:

1. Heat the oil in a medium sauté pan on the stovetop. Add the spinach and half the minced garlic to the pan and sauté for a few minutes, until the spinach has wilted. Remove the sautéed spinach from the pan and set it aside.

2. Preheat the air fryer to 390°F.

3. Cut out a piece of aluminum foil the same size as the bottom of the air fryer basket. Brush the foil circle with olive oil. Shape the dough into a circle and place it on top of the foil. Dock the dough by piercing it several times with a fork. Brush the dough lightly with olive oil and transfer it into the air fryer basket with the foil on the bottom.

4. Air-fry the plain pizza dough for 6 minutes. Turn the dough over, remove the aluminum foil and brush again with olive oil. Air-fry for an additional 4 minutes.

5. Sprinkle the mozzarella and Fontina cheeses over the dough. Top with the spinach and artichoke hearts. Sprinkle the Parmesan cheese and dried oregano on top and drizzle with olive oil. Lower the temperature of the air fryer to 350°F and cook for 8 minutes, until the cheese has melted and is lightly browned. Season to taste with salt and freshly ground black pepper.

Peppered Maple Bacon Knots

Servings: 6

Cooking Time: 8 Minutes

Ingredients:

➢ 1 pound maple smoked center-cut bacon

➢ ¼ cup maple syrup

➢ ¼ cup brown sugar

➢ coarsely cracked black peppercorns

Directions:

1. Tie each bacon strip in a loose knot and place them on a baking sheet.

2. Combine the maple syrup and brown sugar in a bowl. Brush each knot generously with this mixture and sprinkle with coarsely cracked black pepper.

3. Preheat the air fryer to 390°F.

4. Air-fry the bacon knots in batches. Place one layer of knots in the air fryer basket and air-fry for 5 minutes. Turn the bacon knots over and air-fry for an additional 3 minutes.

5. Serve warm.

Strawberry Toast

Servings: 4

Cooking Time: 8 Minutes

Ingredients:

- ➤ 4 slices bread, ½-inch thick
- ➤ butter-flavored cooking spray
- ➤ 1 cup sliced strawberries
- ➤ 1 teaspoon sugar

Directions:

1. Spray one side of each bread slice with butter-flavored cooking spray. Lay slices sprayed side down.
2. Divide the strawberries among the bread slices.
3. Sprinkle evenly with the sugar and place in the air fryer basket in a single layer.
4. Cook at 390°F for 8minutes. The bottom should look brown and crisp and the top should look glazed.

Seasoned Herbed Sourdough Croutons

Servings: 4

Cooking Time: 7 Minutes

Ingredients:

➢ 4 cups cubed sourdough bread, 1-inch cubes (about 8 ounces)

➢ 1 tablespoon olive oil

➢ 1 teaspoon fresh thyme leaves

➢ ¼ – ½ teaspoon salt

➢ freshly ground black pepper

Directions:

1. Combine all ingredients in a bowl and taste to make sure it is seasoned to your liking.

2. Preheat the air fryer to 400°F.

3. Toss the bread cubes into the air fryer and air-fry for 7 minutes, shaking the basket once or twice while they cook.

4. Serve warm or store in an airtight container.

Southern Sweet Cornbread

Servings: 6

Cooking Time: 17 Minutes

Ingredients:

- ➢ cooking spray
- ➢ ½ cup white cornmeal
- ➢ ½ cup flour
- ➢ 2 teaspoons baking powder
- ➢ ½ teaspoon salt
- ➢ 4 teaspoons sugar
- ➢ 1 egg
- ➢ 2 tablespoons oil
- ➢ ½ cup milk

Directions:

1. Preheat air fryer to 360°F.

2. Spray air fryer baking pan with nonstick cooking spray.

3. In a medium bowl, stir together the cornmeal, flour, baking powder, salt, and sugar.

4. In a small bowl, beat together the egg, oil, and milk. Stir into dry ingredients until well combined.

5. Pour batter into prepared baking pan.

6. Cook at 360°F for 17 minutes or until toothpick inserted in center comes out clean or with crumbs clinging.

Scones

Servings: 9

Cooking Time: 8 Minutes Per Batch

Ingredients:

➢ 2 cups self-rising flour, plus ¼ cup for kneading

➢ ⅓ cup granulated sugar

➢ ¼ cup butter, cold

➢ 1 cup milk

Directions:

1. Preheat air fryer at 360°F.

2. In large bowl, stir together flour and sugar.

3. Cut cold butter into tiny cubes, and stir into flour mixture with fork.

4. Stir in milk until soft dough forms.

5. Sprinkle ¼ cup of flour onto wax paper and place dough on top. Knead lightly by folding and turning the dough about 6 to 8 times.

6. Pat dough into a 6 x 6-inch square.

7. Cut into 9 equal squares.

8. Place all squares in air fryer basket or as many as will fit in a single layer, close together but not touching.

9. Cook at 360°F for 8minutes. When done, scones will be lightly browned on top and will spring back when pressed gently with a dull knife.

10. Repeat steps 8 and 9 to cook remaining scones.

Fried Pb&j

Servings: 4

Cooking Time: 8 Minutes

Ingredients:

- ½ cup cornflakes, crushed
- ¼ cup shredded coconut
- 8 slices oat nut bread or any whole-grain, oversize bread
- 6 tablespoons peanut butter
- 2 medium bananas, cut into ½-inch-thick slices
- 6 tablespoons pineapple preserves
- 1 egg, beaten
- oil for misting or cooking spray

Directions:

1. Preheat air fryer to 360°F.

2. In a shallow dish, mix together the cornflake crumbs and coconut.

3. For each sandwich, spread one bread slice with 1½ tablespoons of peanut butter. Top with banana slices. Spread another bread slice with 1½ tablespoons of preserves. Combine to make a sandwich.

4. Using a pastry brush, brush top of sandwich lightly with beaten egg. Sprinkle with about 1½ tablespoons of crumb coating, pressing it in to make it stick. Spray with oil.

5. Turn sandwich over and repeat to coat and spray the other side.

6. Cooking 2 at a time, place sandwiches in air fryer basket and cook for 6 to 7minutes or until coating is golden brown and crispy. If sandwich doesn't brown enough, spray with a little more oil and cook at 390°F for another minute.

7. Cut cooked sandwiches in half and serve warm.

Sweet-hot Pepperoni Pizza

Servings: 2

Cooking Time: 18 Minutes

Ingredients:

➢ 1 (6- to 8-ounce) pizza dough ball*

➢ olive oil

➢ ½ cup pizza sauce

➢ ¾ cup grated mozzarella cheese

➢ ½ cup thick sliced pepperoni

➢ ⅓ cup sliced pickled hot banana peppers

➢ ¼ teaspoon dried oregano

➢ 2 teaspoons honey

Directions:

1. Preheat the air fryer to 390°F.
2. Cut out a piece of aluminum foil the same size as the bottom of the air fryer basket. Brush the foil circle with olive oil. Shape the dough into a circle and place it on top of the foil. Dock the dough by piercing it several times with a fork. Brush the dough lightly with olive oil and transfer it into the air fryer basket with the foil on the bottom.
3. Air-fry the plain pizza dough for 6 minutes. Turn the dough over, remove the aluminum foil and brush again with olive oil. Air-fry for an additional 4 minutes.
4. Spread the pizza sauce on top of the dough and sprinkle the mozzarella cheese over the sauce. Top with the pepperoni, pepper slices and dried oregano. Lower the temperature of the air fryer to 350°F and cook for 8 minutes, until the cheese has melted and lightly browned. Transfer the pizza to a cutting board and drizzle with the honey. Slice and serve.

Southwest Cornbread

Servings: 6

Cooking Time: 18 Minutes

Ingredients:

- cooking spray
- ½ cup yellow cornmeal
- ½ cup flour
- 2 teaspoons baking powder
- ½ teaspoon salt
- ½ cup frozen corn kernels, thawed and drained
- ¼ cup finely chopped onion
- 1 or 2 small jalapeño peppers, seeded and chopped
- 1 egg
- ½ cup milk
- 2 tablespoons melted butter
- 2 ounces sharp Cheddar cheese, grated

Directions:

1. Preheat air fryer to 360°F.
2. Spray air fryer baking pan with nonstick cooking spray.
3. In a medium bowl, stir together the cornmeal, flour, baking powder, and salt.
4. Stir in the corn, onion, and peppers.
5. In a small bowl, beat together the egg, milk, and butter. Stir into dry ingredients until well combined.
6. Spoon half the batter into prepared baking pan, spreading to edges. Top with grated cheese. Spoon remaining batter on top of cheese and gently spread to edges of pan so it completely covers the cheese.
7. Cook at 360°F for 18 minutes, until cornbread is done and top is crispy brown.

Country Gravy

Servings: 2

Cooking Time: 7 Minutes

Ingredients:

- ¼ pound pork sausage, casings removed
- 1 tablespoon butter
- 2 tablespoons flour
- 2 cups whole milk
- ½ teaspoon salt
- freshly ground black pepper
- 1 teaspoon fresh thyme leaves

Directions:

1. Preheat a saucepan over medium heat. Add and brown the sausage, crumbling it into small pieces as it cooks. Add the butter and flour, stirring well to combine. Continue to cook for 2 minutes, stirring constantly.

2. Slowly pour in the milk, whisking as you do, and bring the mixture to a boil to thicken. Season with salt and freshly ground black pepper, lower the heat and simmer until the sauce has thickened to your desired consistency – about 5 minutes. Stir in the fresh thyme, season to taste and serve hot.

Ham And Cheddar Gritters

Servings: 6   Cooking Time: 12 Minutes

Ingredients:

- 4 cups water
- 1 cup quick-cooking grits
- ¼ teaspoon salt
- 2 tablespoons butter
- 2 cups grated Cheddar cheese, divided
- 1 cup finely diced ham

- 1 tablespoon chopped chives
- salt and freshly ground black pepper
- 1 egg, beaten
- 2 cups panko breadcrumbs
- vegetable oil

Directions:

1. Bring the water to a boil in a saucepan. Whisk in the grits and ¼ teaspoon of salt, and cook for 7 minutes until the grits are soft. Remove the pan from the heat and stir in the butter and 1 cup of the grated Cheddar cheese. Transfer the grits to a bowl and let them cool for just 10 to 15 minutes.

2. Stir the ham, chives and the rest of the cheese into the grits and season with salt and pepper to taste. Add the beaten egg and refrigerate the mixture for 30 minutes. (Try not to chill the grits much longer than 30 minutes, or the mixture will be too firm to shape into patties.)

3. While the grit mixture is chilling, make the country gravy and set it aside.

4. Place the panko breadcrumbs in a shallow dish. Measure out ¼-cup portions of the grits mixture and shape them into patties. Coat all sides of the patties with the panko breadcrumbs, patting them with your hands so the crumbs adhere to the patties. You should have about 16 patties. Spray both sides of the patties with oil.

5. Preheat the air fryer to 400°F.

6. In batches of 5 or 6, air-fry the fritters for 8 minutes. Using a flat spatula, flip the fritters over and air-fry for another 4 minutes.

7. Serve hot with country gravy.

Vegetable Side Dishes Recipes

Yellow Squash

Servings: 4   Cooking Time: 10 Minutes

Ingredients:

- 1 large yellow squash (about 1½ cups)
- 2 eggs
- ¼ cup buttermilk
- 1 cup panko breadcrumbs
- ¼ cup white cornmeal
- ½ teaspoon salt
- oil for misting or cooking spray

Directions:

1. Preheat air fryer to 390°F.
2. Cut the squash into ¼-inch slices.
3. In a shallow dish, beat together eggs and buttermilk.
4. In sealable plastic bag or container with lid, combine ¼ cup panko crumbs, white cornmeal, and salt. Shake to mix well.
5. Place the remaining ¾ cup panko crumbs in a separate shallow dish.
6. Dump all the squash slices into the egg/buttermilk mixture. Stir to coat.
7. Remove squash from buttermilk mixture with a slotted spoon, letting excess drip off, and transfer to the panko/cornmeal mixture. Close bag or container and shake well to coat.
8. Remove squash from crumb mixture, letting excess fall off. Return squash to egg/buttermilk mixture, stirring gently to coat. If you need more liquid to coat all the squash, add a little more buttermilk.
9. Remove each squash slice from egg wash and dip in a dish of ¾ cup panko crumbs.
10. Mist squash slices with oil or cooking spray and place in air fryer basket. Squash should be in a single layer, but it's okay if the slices crowd together and overlap a little.
11. Cook at 390°F for 5minutes. Shake basket to break up any that have stuck together. Mist again with oil or spray.
12. Cook 5minutes longer and check. If necessary, mist again with oil and cook an additional two minutes, until squash slices are golden brown and crisp.

Steamboat Shrimp Salad

Servings: 4   Cooking Time: 4 Minutes

Ingredients:

- Steamboat Dressing
- ½ cup mayonnaise
- ½ cup plain yogurt
- 2 teaspoons freshly squeezed lemon juice (no substitutes)
- 2 teaspoons grated lemon rind
- 1 teaspoon dill weed, slightly crushed
- ½ teaspoon hot sauce
- Steamed Shrimp
- 24 small, raw shrimp, peeled and deveined
- 1 teaspoon lemon juice
- ¼ teaspoon Old Bay Seasoning
- Salad
- 8 cups romaine or Bibb lettuce, chopped or torn
- ¼ cup red onion, cut in thin slivers
- 12 black olives, sliced
- 12 cherry or grape tomatoes, halved
- 1 medium avocado, sliced or cut into large chunks

Directions:

1. Combine all dressing ingredients and mix well. Refrigerate while preparing shrimp and salad.
2. Sprinkle raw shrimp with lemon juice and Old Bay Seasoning. Use more Old Bay if you like your shrimp bold and spicy.
3. Pour 4 tablespoons of water in bottom of air fryer.
4. Place shrimp in air fryer basket in single layer.
5. Cook at 390°F for 4 minutes. Remove shrimp from basket and place in refrigerator to cool.
6. Combine all salad ingredients and mix gently. Divide among 4 salad plates or bowls.
7. Top each salad with 6 shrimp and serve with dressing.

Fried Pearl Onions With Balsamic Vinegar And Basil

Servings: 2

Cooking Time: 10 Minutes

Ingredients:

➤ 1 pound fresh pearl onions

➤ 1 tablespoon olive oil

➤ salt and freshly ground black pepper

➤ 1 teaspoon high quality aged balsamic vinegar

➤ 1 tablespoon chopped fresh basil leaves (or mint)

Directions:

1. Preheat the air fryer to 400°F.

2. Decide whether you want to peel the onions before or after they cook. Peeling them ahead of time is a little more laborious. Peeling after they cook is easier, but a little messier since the onions are hot and you may discard more of the onion than you'd like to. If you opt to peel them first, trim the tiny root of the onions off and pinch off any loose papery skins. (It's ok if there are some skins left on the onions.) Toss the pearl onions with the olive oil, salt and freshly ground black pepper.

3. Air-fry for 10 minutes, shaking the basket a couple of times during the cooking process. (If your pearl onions are very large, you may need to add a couple of minutes to this cooking time.)

4. Let the onions cool slightly and then slip off any remaining skins.

5. Toss the onions with the balsamic vinegar and basil and serve.

Perfect Asparagus

Servings: 3

Cooking Time: 10 Minutes

Ingredients:

➢ 1 pound Very thin asparagus spears

➢ 2 tablespoons Olive oil

➢ 1 teaspoon Coarse sea salt or kosher salt

➢ ¾ teaspoon Finely grated lemon zest

Directions:

1. Preheat the air fryer to 400°F.

2. Trim just enough off the bottom of the asparagus spears so they'll fit in the basket. Put the spears on a large plate and drizzle them with some of the olive oil. Turn them over and drizzle more olive oil, working to get all the spears coated.

3. When the machine is at temperature, place the spears in one direction in the basket. They may be touching. Air-fry for 10 minutes, tossing and rearranging the spears twice, until tender.

4. Dump the contents of the basket on a serving platter. Spread out the spears. Sprinkle them with the salt and lemon zest while still warm. Serve at once.

Parmesan Garlic Fries

Servings: 4

Cooking Time: 20 Minutes

Ingredients:

➢ 2 medium Yukon gold potatoes, washed

➢ 1 tablespoon extra-virgin olive oil

➢ 1 garlic clove, minced

➢ 2 tablespoons finely grated parmesan cheese

➢ ¼ teaspoon black pepper

➢ ¼ teaspoon salt

➢ 1 tablespoon freshly chopped parsley

Directions:

1. Preheat the air fryer to 400°F.

2. Slice the potatoes into long strips about ¼-inch thick. In a large bowl, toss the potatoes with the olive oil, garlic, cheese, pepper, and salt.

3. Place the fries into the air fryer basket and cook for 4 minutes; shake the basket and cook another 4 minutes.

4. Remove and serve warm.

Zucchini Fries

Servings: 3

Cooking Time: 12 Minutes

Ingredients:

➢ 1 large Zucchini

➢ ½ cup All-purpose flour or tapioca flour

➢ 2 Large egg(s), well beaten

➢ 1 cup Seasoned Italian-style dried bread crumbs (gluten-free, if a concern)

➢ Olive oil spray

Directions:

1. Preheat the air fryer to 400°F.

2. Trim the zucchini into a long rectangular block, taking off the ends and four "sides" to make this shape. Cut the block lengthwise into ½-inch-thick slices. Lay these slices flat and cut in half widthwise. Slice each of these pieces into ½-inch-thick batons.

3. Set up and fill three shallow soup plates or small pie plates on your counter: one for the flour, one for the beaten egg(s), and one for the bread crumbs.

4. Set a zucchini baton in the flour and turn it several times to coat all sides. Gently shake off any excess flour, then dip it in the egg(s), turning it to coat. Let any excess egg slip back into the rest, then set the baton in the bread crumbs and turn it several times, pressing gently to coat all sides, even the ends. Set aside on a cutting board and continue coating the remainder of the batons in the same way.

5. Lightly coat the batons on all sides with olive oil spray. Set them in two flat layers in the basket, the top layer at a 90-degree angle to the bottom one, with a little air space between the batons in each layer. In the end, the whole thing will look like a crosshatch pattern. Air-fry undisturbed for 6 minutes.

6. Use kitchen tongs to gently rearrange the batons so that any covered parts are now uncovered. The batons no longer need to be in a crosshatch pattern. Continue air-frying undisturbed for 6 minutes, or until lightly browned and crisp.

7. Gently pour the contents of the basket onto a wire rack. Spread the batons out and cool for only a minute or two before serving.

Moroccan Cauliflower

Servings: 6

Cooking Time: 15 Minutes

Ingredients:

- ➢ 1 tablespoon curry powder
- ➢ 2 teaspoons smoky paprika
- ➢ ½ teaspoon ground cumin
- ➢ ½ teaspoon salt
- ➢ 1 head cauliflower, cut into bite-size pieces
- ➢ ¼ cup red wine vinegar
- ➢ 2 tablespoons extra-virgin olive oil
- ➢ 2 tablespoons chopped parsley

Directions:

1. Preheat the air fryer to 370°F.

2. In a large bowl, mix the curry powder, paprika, cumin, and salt. Add the cauliflower and stir to coat. Pour the red wine vinegar over the top and continue stirring.

3. Place the cauliflower into the air fryer basket; drizzle olive oil over the top.

4. Cook the cauliflower for 5 minutes, toss, and cook another 5 minutes. Raise the temperature to 400°F and continue cooking for 4 to 6 minutes, or until crispy.

Cheesy Potato Pot

Servings: 4

Cooking Time: 13 Minutes

Ingredients:

- 3 cups cubed red potatoes (unpeeled, cut into ½-inch cubes)
- ½ teaspoon garlic powder
- salt and pepper
- 1 tablespoon oil
- chopped chives for garnish (optional)
- Sauce
- 2 tablespoons milk
- 1 tablespoon butter
- 2 ounces sharp Cheddar cheese, grated
- 1 tablespoon sour cream

Directions:

1. Place potato cubes in large bowl and sprinkle with garlic, salt, and pepper. Add oil and stir to coat well.

2. Cook at 390°F for 13 minutes or until potatoes are tender. Stir every 4 or 5minutes during cooking time.

3. While potatoes are cooking, combine milk and butter in a small saucepan. Warm over medium-low heat to melt butter. Add cheese and stir until it melts. The melted cheese will remain separated from the milk mixture. Remove from heat until potatoes are done.

4. When ready to serve, add sour cream to cheese mixture and stir over medium-low heat just until warmed. Place cooked potatoes in serving bowl. Pour sauce over potatoes and stir to combine.

5. Garnish with chives if desired.

Crispy Brussels Sprouts

Servings: 3

Cooking Time: 12 Minutes

Ingredients:

➢ 1¼ pounds Medium, 2-inch-in-length Brussels sprouts

➢ 1½ tablespoons Olive oil

➢ ¾ teaspoon Table salt

Directions:

1. Preheat the air fryer to 400°F.

2. Halve each Brussels sprout through the stem end, pulling off and discarding any discolored outer leaves. Put the sprout halves in a large bowl, add the oil and salt, and stir well to coat evenly, until the Brussels sprouts are glistening.

3. When the machine is at temperature, scrape the contents of the bowl into the basket, gently spreading the Brussels sprout halves into as close to one layer as possible. Air-fry for 12 minutes, gently tossing and rearranging the vegetables twice to get all covered or touching parts exposed to the air currents, until crisp and browned at the edges.

4. Gently pour the contents of the basket onto a wire rack. Cool for a minute or two before serving.

Smashed Fried Baby Potatoes

Servings: 3

Cooking Time: 18 Minutes

Ingredients:

- 1½ pounds baby red or baby Yukon gold potatoes
- ¼ cup butter, melted
- 1 teaspoon olive oil
- ½ teaspoon paprika
- 1 teaspoon dried parsley
- salt and freshly ground black pepper
- 2 scallions, finely chopped

Directions:

1. Bring a large pot of salted water to a boil. Add the potatoes and boil for 18 minutes or until the potatoes are fork-tender.

2. Drain the potatoes and transfer them to a cutting board to cool slightly. Spray or brush the bottom of a drinking glass with a little oil. Smash or flatten the potatoes by pressing the glass down on each potato slowly. Try not to completely flatten the potato or smash it so hard that it breaks apart.

3. Combine the melted butter, olive oil, paprika, and parsley together.

4. Preheat the air fryer to 400°F.

5. Spray the bottom of the air fryer basket with oil and transfer one layer of the smashed potatoes into the basket. Brush with some of the butter mixture and season generously with salt and freshly ground black pepper.

6. Air-fry at 400°F for 10 minutes. Carefully flip the potatoes over and air-fry for an additional 8 minutes until crispy and lightly browned.

7. Keep the potatoes warm in a 170°F oven or tent with aluminum foil while you cook the second batch. Sprinkle minced scallions over the potatoes and serve warm.

Beef ， Pork & Lamb Recipes

Meatball Subs

Servings: 4   Cooking Time: 11 Minutes

Ingredients:

- Marinara Sauce
- 1 15-ounce can diced tomatoes
- 1 teaspoon garlic powder
- 1 teaspoon dried basil
- ½ teaspoon oregano
- ⅛ teaspoon salt
- 1 tablespoon robust olive oil
- Meatballs
- ¼ pound ground turkey
- ¾ pound very lean ground beef
- 1 tablespoon milk
- ½ cup torn bread pieces
- 1 egg
- ¼ teaspoon salt
- ½ teaspoon dried onion

- 1 teaspoon garlic powder
- ¼ teaspoon smoked paprika
- ¼ teaspoon crushed red pepper
- 1½ teaspoons dried parsley
- ¼ teaspoon oregano
- 2 teaspoons Worcestershire sauce
- Sandwiches
- 4 large whole-grain sub or hoagie rolls, split
- toppings, sliced or chopped:
- mushrooms
- jalapeño or banana peppers
- red or green bell pepper
- red onions
- grated cheese

Directions:

1. Place all marinara ingredients in saucepan and bring to a boil. Lower heat and simmer 10minutes, uncovered.

2. Combine all meatball ingredients in large bowl and stir. Mixture should be well blended but don't overwork it. Excessive mixing will toughen the meatballs.

3. Divide meat into 16 equal portions and shape into balls.

4. Cook the balls at 360°F until meat is done and juices run clear, about 11 minutes.

5. While meatballs are cooking, taste marinara. If you prefer stronger flavors, add more seasoning and simmer another 5minutes.

6. When meatballs finish cooking, drain them on paper towels.

7. To assemble subs, place 4 meatballs on each sub roll, spoon sauce over meat, and add preferred toppings. Serve with additional marinara for dipping.

Crispy Pierogi With Kielbasa And Onions

Servings: 3

Cooking Time: 20 Minutes

Ingredients:

➢ 6 Frozen potato and cheese pierogi, thawed (about 12 pierogi to 1 pound)

➢ ½ pound Smoked kielbasa, sliced into ½-inch-thick rounds

➢ ¾ cup Very roughly chopped sweet onion, preferably Vidalia

➢ Vegetable oil spray

Directions:

1. Preheat the air fryer to 375°F .

2. Put the pierogi, kielbasa rounds, and onion in a large bowl. Coat them with vegetable oil spray, toss well, spray again, and toss until everything is glistening.

3. When the machine is at temperature, dump the contents of the bowl it into the basket. (Items may be leaning against each other and even on top of each other.) Air-fry, tossing and rearranging everything twice so that all covered surfaces get exposed, for 20 minutes, or until the sausages have begun to brown and the pierogi are crisp.

4. Pour the contents of the basket onto a serving platter. Wait a minute or two just to take make sure nothing's searing hot before serving.

Better-than-chinese-take-out Pork Ribs

Servings: 3

Cooking Time: 35 Minutes

Ingredients:

➢ 1½ tablespoons Hoisin sauce (see here; gluten-free, if a concern)

➢ 1½ tablespoons Regular or low-sodium soy sauce or gluten-free tamari sauce

➢ 1½ tablespoons Shaoxing (Chinese cooking rice wine), dry sherry, or white grape juice

➢ 1½ teaspoons Minced garlic

➢ ¾ teaspoon Ground dried ginger

➢ ¾ teaspoon Ground white pepper

➢ 1½ pounds Pork baby back rib rack(s), cut into 2-bone pieces

Directions:

1. Mix the hoisin sauce, soy or tamari sauce, Shaoxing or its substitute, garlic, ginger, and white pepper in a large bowl. Add the rib sections and stir well to coat. Cover and refrigerate for at least 2 hours or up to 24 hours, stirring the rib sections in the marinade occasionally.

2. Preheat the air fryer to 350°F . Set the ribs in their bowl on the counter as the machine heats.

3. When the machine is at temperature, set the rib pieces on their sides in a single layer in the basket with as much air space between them as possible. Air-fry for 35 minutes, turning and rearranging the pieces once, until deeply browned and sizzling.

4. Use kitchen tongs to transfer the rib pieces to a large serving bowl or platter. Wait a minute or two before serving them so the meat can reabsorb some of its own juices.

Pork Cutlets With Aloha Salsa

Servings: 4   Cooking Time: 9 Minutes

Ingredients:

- Aloha Salsa
- 1 cup fresh pineapple, chopped in small pieces
- ¼ cup red onion, finely chopped
- ¼ cup green or red bell pepper, chopped
- ½ teaspoon ground cinnamon
- 1 teaspoon low-sodium soy sauce
- ⅛ teaspoon crushed red pepper
- ⅛ teaspoon ground black pepper
- 2 eggs
- 2 tablespoons milk
- ¼ cup flour
- ¼ cup panko breadcrumbs
- 4 teaspoons sesame seeds
- 1 pound boneless, thin pork cutlets (⅜- to ½-inch thick)
- lemon pepper and salt
- ¼ cup cornstarch
- oil for misting or cooking spray

Directions:

1. In a medium bowl, stir together all ingredients for salsa. Cover and refrigerate while cooking pork.
2. Preheat air fryer to 390°F.
3. Beat together eggs and milk in shallow dish.
4. In another shallow dish, mix together the flour, panko, and sesame seeds.
5. Sprinkle pork cutlets with lemon pepper and salt to taste. Most lemon pepper seasoning contains salt, so go easy adding extra.
6. Dip pork cutlets in cornstarch, egg mixture, and then panko coating. Spray both sides with oil or cooking spray.
7. Cook cutlets for 3minutes. Turn cutlets over, spraying both sides, and continue cooking for 6 minutes or until well done.
8. Serve fried cutlets with salsa on the side.

Air-fried Roast Beef With Rosemary Roasted Potatoes

Servings: 8

Cooking Time: 60 Minutes

Ingredients:

➤ 1 (5-pound) top sirloin roast

➤ salt and freshly ground black pepper

➤ 1 teaspoon dried thyme

➤ 2 pounds red potatoes, halved or quartered

➤ 2 teaspoons olive oil

➤ 1 teaspoon very finely chopped fresh rosemary, plus more for garnish

Directions:

1. Start by making sure your roast will fit into the air fryer basket without touching the top element. Trim it if you have to in order to get it to fit nicely in your air fryer. (You can always save the trimmings for another use, like a beef sandwich.)

2. Preheat the air fryer to 360°F.

3. Season the beef all over with salt, pepper and thyme. Transfer the seasoned roast to the air fryer basket.

4. Air-fry at 360°F for 20 minutes. Turn the roast over and continue to air-fry at 360°F for another 20 minutes.

5. Toss the potatoes with the olive oil, salt, pepper and fresh rosemary. Turn the roast over again in the air fryer basket and toss the potatoes in around the sides of the roast. Air-fry the roast and potatoes at 360°F for another 20 minutes. Check the internal temperature of the roast with an instant-read thermometer, and continue to roast until the beef is 5° lower than your desired degree of doneness. (Rare – 130°F, Medium – 150°F, Well done – 170°F.) Let the roast rest for 5 to 10 minutes before slicing and serving. While the roast is resting, continue to air-fry the potatoes if desired for extra browning and crispiness.

6. Slice the roast and serve with the potatoes, adding a little more fresh rosemary if desired.

Barbecue-style Beef Cube Steak

Servings: 2

Cooking Time: 14 Minutes

Ingredients:

➢ 2 4-ounce beef cube steak(s)

➢ 2 cups (about 8 ounces) Fritos (original flavor) or a generic corn chip equivalent, crushed to crumbs (see here)

➢ 6 tablespoons Purchased smooth barbecue sauce, any flavor (gluten-free, if a concern)

Directions:

1. Preheat the air fryer to 375°F .

2. Spread the Fritos crumbs in a shallow soup plate or a small pie plate. Rub the barbecue sauce onto both sides of the steak(s). Dredge the steak(s) in the Fritos crumbs to coat well and thoroughly, turning several times and pressing down to get the little bits to adhere to the meat.

3. When the machine is at temperature, set the steak(s) in the basket. Leave as much air space between them as possible if you're working with more than one piece of beef. Air-fry undisturbed for 12 minutes, or until lightly brown and crunchy. If the machine is at 360°F, you may need to add 2 minutes to the cooking time.

4. Use kitchen tongs to transfer the steak(s) to a wire rack. Cool for 5 minutes before serving.

Steakhouse Filets Mignons

Servings: 3

Cooking Time: 12-15 Minutes

Ingredients:

- ¾ ounce Dried porcini mushrooms
- ¼ teaspoon Granulated white sugar
- ¼ teaspoon Ground white pepper
- ¼ teaspoon Table salt
- 6 ¼-pound filets mignons or beef tenderloin steaks
- 6 Thin-cut bacon strips (gluten-free, if a concern)

Directions:

1. Preheat the air fryer to 400°F.

2. Grind the dried mushrooms in a clean spice grinder until powdery. Add the sugar, white pepper, and salt. Grind to blend.

3. Rub this mushroom mixture into both cut sides of each filet. Wrap the circumference of each filet with a strip of bacon. (It will loop around the beef about 1½ times.)

4. Set the filets mignons in the basket on their sides with the bacon seam side down. Do not let the filets touch; keep at least ¼ inch open between them. Air-fry undisturbed for 12 minutes for rare, or until an instant-read meat thermometer inserted into the center of a filet registers 125°F (not USDA-approved); 13 minutes for medium-rare, or until an instant-read meat thermometer inserted into the center of a filet registers 132°F (not USDA-approved); or 15 minutes for medium, or until an instant-read meat thermometer inserted into the center of a filet registers 145°F (USDA-approved).

5. Use kitchen tongs to transfer the filets to a wire rack, setting them cut side down. Cool for 5 minutes before serving.

Blackberry Bbq Glazed Country-style Ribs

Servings: 2

Cooking Time: 40 Minutes

Ingredients:

- ½ cup + 2 tablespoons sherry or Madeira wine, divided
- 1 pound boneless country-style pork ribs
- salt and freshly ground black pepper
- 1 tablespoon Chinese 5-spice powder
- ¼ cup blackberry preserves
- ¼ cup hoisin sauce*
- 1 clove garlic, minced
- 1 generous tablespoon grated fresh ginger
- 2 scallions, chopped
- 1 tablespoon sesame seeds, toasted

Directions:

1. Preheat the air fryer to 330°F and pour ½ cup of the sherry into the bottom of the air fryer drawer.
2. Season the ribs with salt, pepper and the 5-spice powder.
3. Air-fry the ribs at 330°F for 20 minutes, turning them over halfway through the cooking time.
4. While the ribs are cooking, make the sauce. Combine the remaining sherry, blackberry preserves, hoisin sauce, garlic and ginger in a small saucepan. Bring to a simmer on the stovetop for a few minutes, until the sauce thickens.
5. When the time is up on the air fryer, turn the ribs over, pour a little sauce on the ribs and air-fry for another 10 minutes at 330°F. Turn the ribs over again, pour on more of the sauce and air-fry at 330°F for a final 10 minutes.
6. Let the ribs rest for at least 5 minutes before serving them warm with a little more glaze brushed on and the scallions and sesame seeds sprinkled on top.

Lamb Meatballs With Quick Tomato Sauce

Servings: 4   Cooking Time: 8 Minutes

Ingredients:

- ½ small onion, finely diced
- 1 clove garlic, minced
- 1 pound ground lamb
- 2 tablespoons fresh parsley, finely chopped (plus more for garnish)
- 2 teaspoons fresh oregano, finely chopped
- 2 tablespoons milk
- 1 egg yolk
- salt and freshly ground black pepper
- ½ cup crumbled feta cheese, for garnish
- Tomato Sauce:
- 2 tablespoons butter
- 1 clove garlic, smashed
- pinch crushed red pepper flakes
- ¼ teaspoon ground cinnamon
- 1 (28-ounce) can crushed tomatoes
- salt, to taste

Directions:

1. Combine all ingredients for the meatballs in a large bowl and mix just until everything is combined. Shape the mixture into 1½-inch balls or shape the meat between two spoons to make quenelles (little three-sided footballs).

2. Preheat the air fryer to 400°F.

3. While the air fryer is Preheating, start the quick tomato sauce. Place the butter, garlic and red pepper flakes in a sauté pan and heat over medium heat on the stovetop. Let the garlic sizzle a little, but before the butter starts to brown, add the cinnamon and tomatoes. Bring to a simmer and simmer for 15 minutes. Season to taste with salt (but not too much as the feta that you will be sprinkling on at the end will be salty).

4. Brush the bottom of the air fryer basket with a little oil and transfer the meatballs to the air fryer basket in one layer, air-frying in batches if necessary.

5. Air-fry at 400°F for 8 minutes, giving the basket a shake once during the cooking process to turn the meatballs over.

6. To serve, spoon a pool of the tomato sauce onto plates and add the meatballs in a decorative manner. Sprinkle the feta cheese on top and garnish with more fresh parsley. Serve immediately.

Stuffed Bell Peppers

Servings: 4

Cooking Time: 10 Minutes

Ingredients:

- ¼ pound lean ground pork
- ¾ pound lean ground beef
- ¼ cup onion, minced
- 1 15-ounce can Red Gold crushed tomatoes
- 1 teaspoon Worcestershire sauce
- 1 teaspoon barbeque seasoning
- 1 teaspoon honey
- ½ teaspoon dried basil
- ½ cup cooked brown rice
- ½ teaspoon garlic powder
- ½ teaspoon oregano
- ½ teaspoon salt
- 2 small bell peppers

Directions:

1. Place pork, beef, and onion in air fryer baking pan and cook at 360°F for 5minutes.

2. Stir to break apart chunks and cook 3 more minutes. Continue cooking and stirring in 2-minute intervals until meat is well done. Remove from pan and drain.

3. In a small saucepan, combine the tomatoes, Worcestershire, barbeque seasoning, honey, and basil. Stir well to mix in honey and seasonings.

4. In a large bowl, combine the cooked meat mixture, rice, garlic powder, oregano, and salt. Add ¼ cup of the seasoned crushed tomatoes. Stir until well mixed.

5. Cut peppers in half and remove stems and seeds.

6. Stuff each pepper half with one fourth of the meat mixture.

7. Place the peppers in air fryer basket and cook for 10 minutes, until peppers are crisp tender.

8. Heat remaining tomato sauce. Serve peppers with warm sauce spooned over top.

Red Curry Flank Steak

Servings: 4

Cooking Time: 18 Minutes

Ingredients:

- ➤ 3 tablespoons red curry paste
- ➤ ¼ cup olive oil
- ➤ 2 teaspoons grated fresh ginger
- ➤ 2 tablespoons soy sauce
- ➤ 2 tablespoons rice wine vinegar
- ➤ 3 scallions, minced
- ➤ 1½ pounds flank steak
- ➤ fresh cilantro (or parsley) leaves

Directions:

1. Mix the red curry paste, olive oil, ginger, soy sauce, rice vinegar and scallions together in a bowl. Place the flank steak in a shallow glass dish and pour half the marinade over the steak. Pierce the steak several times with a fork or meat tenderizer to let the marinade penetrate the meat. Turn the steak over, pour the remaining marinade over the top and pierce the steak several times again. Cover and marinate the steak in the refrigerator for 6 to 8 hours.

2. When you are ready to cook, remove the steak from the refrigerator and let it sit at room temperature for 30 minutes.

3. Preheat the air fryer to 400°F.

4. Cut the flank steak in half so that it fits more easily into the air fryer and transfer both pieces to the air fryer basket. Pour the marinade over the steak. Air-fry for 18 minutes, depending on your preferred degree of doneness of the steak (12 minutes = medium rare). Flip the steak over halfway through the cooking time.

5. When your desired degree of doneness has been reached, remove the steak to a cutting board and let it rest for 5 minutes before slicing. Thinly slice the flank steak against the grain of the meat. Transfer the slices to a serving platter, pour any juice from the bottom of the air fryer over the sliced flank steak and sprinkle the fresh cilantro on top.

Pizza Tortilla Rolls

Servings: 4

Cooking Time: 8 Minutes

Ingredients:

- 1 teaspoon butter
- ½ medium onion, slivered
- ½ red or green bell pepper, julienned
- 4 ounces fresh white mushrooms, chopped
- 8 flour tortillas (6- or 7-inch size)
- ½ cup pizza sauce
- 8 thin slices deli ham
- 24 pepperoni slices (about 1½ ounces)
- 1 cup shredded mozzarella cheese (about 4 ounces)
- oil for misting or cooking spray

Directions:

1. Place butter, onions, bell pepper, and mushrooms in air fryer baking pan. Cook at 390°F for 3minutes. Stir and cook 4 minutes longer until just crisp and tender. Remove pan and set aside.

2. To assemble rolls, spread about 2 teaspoons of pizza sauce on one half of each tortilla. Top with a slice of ham and 3 slices of pepperoni. Divide sautéed vegetables among tortillas and top with cheese.

3. Roll up tortillas, secure with toothpicks if needed, and spray with oil.

4. Place 4 rolls in air fryer basket and cook for 4minutes. Turn and cook 4 minutes, until heated through and lightly browned.

5. Repeat step 4 to cook remaining pizza rolls.

Lamb Chops

Servings: 2

Cooking Time: 20 Minutes

Ingredients:

- 2 teaspoons oil
- ½ teaspoon ground rosemary
- ½ teaspoon lemon juice
- 1 pound lamb chops, approximately 1-inch thick
- salt and pepper
- cooking spray

Directions:

1. Mix the oil, rosemary, and lemon juice together and rub into all sides of the lamb chops. Season to taste with salt and pepper.

2. For best flavor, cover lamb chops and allow them to rest in the fridge for 20 minutes.

3. Spray air fryer basket with nonstick spray and place lamb chops in it.

4. Cook at 360°F for approximately 20minutes. This will cook chops to medium. The meat will be juicy but have no remaining pink. Cook for a minute or two longer for well done chops. For rare chops, stop cooking after about 12minutes and check for doneness.

Appetizers And Snacks

Beef Steak Sliders

Servings: 8

Cooking Time: 22 Minutes

Ingredients:

- ➢ 1 pound top sirloin steaks, about ¾-inch thick
- ➢ salt and pepper
- ➢ 2 large onions, thinly sliced
- ➢ 1 tablespoon extra-light olive oil
- ➢ 8 slider buns
- ➢ Horseradish Mayonnaise
- ➢ 1 cup light mayonnaise
- ➢ 4 teaspoons prepared horseradish
- ➢ 2 teaspoons Worcestershire sauce
- ➢ 1 teaspoon coarse brown mustard

Directions:

1. Place steak in air fryer basket and cook at 390°F for 6minutes. Turn and cook 6 more minutes for medium rare. If you prefer your steak medium, continue cooking for 3 minutes.

2. While the steak is cooking, prepare the Horseradish Mayonnaise by mixing all ingredients together.

3. When steak is cooked, remove from air fryer, sprinkle with salt and pepper to taste, and set aside to rest.

4. Toss the onion slices with the oil and place in air fryer basket. Cook at 390°F for 7 minutes, until onion rings are soft and browned.

5. Slice steak into very thin slices.

6. Spread slider buns with the horseradish mayo and pile on the meat and onions. Serve with remaining horseradish dressing for dipping.

Cherry Chipotle Bbq Chicken Wings

Servings: 2

Cooking Time: 12 Minutes

Ingredients:

- 1 teaspoon smoked paprika
- ½ teaspoon dry mustard powder
- 1 teaspoon dried oregano
- 1 teaspoon dried thyme
- ½ teaspoon chili powder
- 1 teaspoon salt
- 2 pounds chicken wings
- vegetable oil or spray
- salt and freshly ground black pepper
- 1 to 2 tablespoons chopped chipotle peppers in adobo sauce
- ⅓ cup cherry preserves ¼ cup tomato ketchup

Directions:

1. Combine the first six ingredients in a large bowl. Prepare the chicken wings by cutting off the wing tips and discarding (or freezing for chicken stock). Divide the drumettes from the win-gettes by cutting through the joint. Place the chicken wing pieces in the bowl with the spice mix. Toss or shake well to coat.

2. Preheat the air fryer to 400°F.

3. Spray the wings lightly with the vegetable oil and air-fry the wings in two batches for 10 minutes per batch, shaking the basket halfway through the cooking process. When both batches are done, toss all the wings back into the basket for another 2 minutes to heat through and finish cooking.

4. While the wings are air-frying, combine the chopped chipotle peppers, cherry preserves and ketchup in a bowl.

5. Remove the wings from the air fryer, toss them in the cherry chipotle BBQ sauce and serve with napkins!

Mozzarella Sticks

Servings: 4

Cooking Time: 5 Minutes

Ingredients:

➤ 1 egg

➤ 1 tablespoon water

➤ 8 eggroll wraps

➤ 8 mozzarella string cheese "sticks"

➤ sauce for dipping

Directions:

1. Beat together egg and water in a small bowl.

2. Lay out egg roll wraps and moisten edges with egg wash.

3. Place one piece of string cheese on each wrap near one end.

4. Fold in sides of egg roll wrap over ends of cheese, and then roll up.

5. Brush outside of wrap with egg wash and press gently to seal well.

6. Place in air fryer basket in single layer and cook 390°F for 5 minutes. Cook an additional 1 or 2minutes, if necessary, until they are golden brown and crispy.

7. Serve with your favorite dipping sauce.

Spanakopita Spinach, Feta And Pine Nut Phyllo Bites

Servings: 8   Cooking Time: 10 Minutes

Ingredients:

- ½ (10-ounce) package frozen spinach, thawed and squeezed dry (about 1 cup)
- ¾ cup crumbled feta cheese
- ¼ cup grated Parmesan cheese
- ¼ cup pine nuts, toasted
- ⅛ teaspoon ground nutmeg
- 1 egg, lightly beaten
- ½ teaspoon salt
- freshly ground black pepper
- 6 sheets phyllo dough
- ½ cup butter, melted

Directions:

1. Combine the spinach, cheeses, pine nuts, nutmeg and egg in a bowl. Season with salt and freshly ground black pepper.

2. While building the phyllo triangles, always keep the dough sheets you are not working with covered with plastic wrap and a damp clean kitchen towel. Remove one sheet of the phyllo and place it on a flat surface. Brush the phyllo sheet with melted butter and then layer another sheet of phyllo on top. Brush the second sheet of phyllo with butter. Cut the layered phyllo sheets into 6 strips, about 2½- to 3-inches wide.

3. Place a heaping tablespoon of the spinach filling at the end of each strip of dough. Fold the bottom right corner of the strip over the filling towards the left edge of the strip to make a triangle. Continue to fold the phyllo dough around the spinach as you would fold a flag, making triangle after triangle. Brush the outside of the phyllo triangle with more melted butter and set it aside until you've finished the 6 strips of dough, making 6 triangles.

4. Preheat the air fryer to 350°F.

5. Transfer the first six phyllo triangles to the air fryer basket and air-fry for 5 minutes. Turn the triangles over and air-fry for another 5 minutes.

6. While the first batch of triangles is air-frying, build another set of triangles and air-fry in the same manner. You should do three batches total. These can be warmed in the air fryer for a minute or two just before serving if you like.

Grilled Cheese Sandwich

Servings: 2

Cooking Time: 5 Minutes

Ingredients:

➢ 4 slices bread

➢ 4 ounces Cheddar cheese slices

➢ 2 teaspoons butter or oil

Directions:

1. Lay the four cheese slices on two of the bread slices and top with the remaining two slices of bread.

2. Brush both sides with butter or oil and cut the sandwiches in rectangular halves.

3. Place in air fryer basket and cook at 390°F for 5minutes until the outside is crisp and the cheese melts.

Crispy Tofu Bites

Servings: 4

Cooking Time: 20 Minutes

Ingredients:

➢ 1 pound Extra firm unflavored tofu

➢ Vegetable oil spray

Directions:

1. Wrap the piece of tofu in a triple layer of paper towels. Place it on a wooden cutting board and set a large pot on top of it to press out excess moisture. Set aside for 10 minutes.

2. Preheat the air fryer to 400°F.

3. Remove the pot and unwrap the tofu. Cut it into 1-inch cubes. Place these in a bowl and coat them generously with vegetable oil spray. Toss gently, then spray generously again before tossing, until all are glistening.

4. Gently pour the tofu pieces into the basket, spread them into as close to one layer as possible, and air-fry for 20 minutes, using kitchen tongs to gently rearrange the pieces at the 7- and 14-minute marks, until light brown and crisp.

5. Gently pour the tofu pieces onto a wire rack. Cool for 5 minutes before serving warm.

Crunchy Spicy Chickpeas

Servings: 6

Cooking Time: 12 Minutes

Ingredients:

- ➤ 2½ cups Canned chickpeas, drained and rinsed
- ➤ 2½ tablespoons Vegetable or canola oil
- ➤ up to 1 tablespoon Cajun or jerk dried seasoning blend (see here for a Cajun blend, here for a jerk blend)
- ➤ up to ¾ teaspoon Table salt (optional)

Directions:

1. Preheat the air fryer to 400°F.

2. Toss the chickpeas, oil, seasoning blend, and salt (if using) in a large bowl until the chickpeas are evenly coated.

3. When the machine is at temperature, pour the chickpeas into the basket. Air-fry for 12 minutes, removing the basket at the 4- and 8-minute marks to toss and rearrange the chickpeas, until very aromatic and perhaps sizzling but not burned.

4. Pour the chickpeas into a large serving bowl. Cool for a couple of minutes, gently stirring once, before you dive in.

Corn Dog Bites

Servings: 3

Cooking Time: 12 Minutes

Ingredients:

➤ 3 cups Purchased cornbread stuffing mix

➤ ⅓ cup All-purpose flour

➤ 2 Large egg(s), well beaten

➤ 3 Hot dogs, cut into 2-inch pieces (vegetarian hot dogs, if preferred)

➤ Vegetable oil spray

Directions:

1. Preheat the air fryer to 375°F .

2. Put the cornbread stuffing mix in a food processor. Cover and pulse to grind into a mixture like fine bread crumbs.

3. Set up and fill three shallow soup plates or small pie plates on your counter: one for the flour, one for the egg(s), and one for the stuffing mix crumbs.

4. Dip a hot dog piece in the flour to coat it completely, then gently shake off any excess. Dip the hot dog piece into the egg(s) and gently roll it around to coat all surfaces, then pick it up and allow any excess egg to slip back into the rest. Set the hot dog piece in the stuffing mix crumbs and roll it gently to coat it evenly and well on all sides, even the ends. Set it aside on a cutting board and continue dipping and coating the remaining hot dog pieces.

5. Give the coated hot dog pieces a generous coating of vegetable oil spray on all sides, then set them in the basket in one layer with some space between them. Air-fry undisturbed for 10 minutes, or until golden brown and crunchy. (You'll need to add 2 minutes in the air fryer if the temperature is at 360°F.)

6. Use a nonstick-safe spatula, and perhaps a flatware fork for balance, to transfer the corn dog bites to a wire rack. Cool for 5 minutes before serving.

Beet Chips

Servings: 4

Cooking Time: 20 Minutes

Ingredients:

- ➢ 2 large red beets, washed and skinned
- ➢ 1 tablespoon avocado oil
- ➢ ¼ teaspoon salt

Directions:

1. Preheat the air fryer to 330°F.

2. Using a mandolin or sharp knife, slice the beets in ⅛-inch slices. Place them in a bowl of water and let them soak for 30 minutes. Drain the water and pat the beets dry with a paper towel or kitchen cloth.

3. In a medium bowl, toss the beets with avocado oil and sprinkle them with salt.

4. Lightly spray the air fryer basket with olive oil mist and place the beet chips into the basket. To allow for even cooking, don't overlap the beets; cook in batches if necessary.

5. Cook the beet chips 15 to 20 minutes, shaking the basket every 5 minutes, until the outer edges of the beets begin to flip up like a chip. Remove from the basket and serve warm. Repeat with the remaining chips until they're all cooked.

Classic Chicken Wings

Servings: 8

Cooking Time: 20 Minutes

Ingredients:

- ➢ 16 chicken wings
- ➢ ¼ cup all-purpose flour
- ➢ ¼ teaspoon garlic powder
- ➢ ¼ teaspoon paprika
- ➢ ½ teaspoon salt
- ➢ ½ teaspoon black pepper
- ➢ ¼ cup butter
- ➢ ½ cup hot sauce
- ➢ ½ teaspoon Worcestershire sauce
- ➢ 2 ounces crumbled blue cheese, for garnish

Directions:

1. Preheat the air fryer to 380°F.

2. Pat the chicken wings dry with paper towels.

3. In a medium bowl, mix together the flour, garlic powder, paprika, salt, and pepper. Toss the chicken wings with the flour mixture, dusting off any excess.

4. Place the chicken wings in the air fryer basket, making sure that the chicken wings aren't touching. Cook the chicken wings for 10 minutes, turn over, and cook another 5 minutes. Raise the temperature to 400°F and continue crisping the chicken wings for an additional 3 to 5 minutes.

5. Meanwhile, in a microwave-safe bowl, melt the butter and hot sauce for 1 to 2 minutes in the microwave. Remove from the microwave and stir in the Worcestershire sauce.

6. When the chicken wings have cooked, immediately transfer the chicken wings into the hot sauce mixture. Serve the coated chicken wings on a plate, and top with crumbled blue cheese.

Muffuletta Sliders

Servings: 8

Cooking Time: 7 Minutes

Ingredients:

- ¼ pound thin-sliced deli ham
- ¼ pound thin-sliced pastrami
- 4 ounces low-fat mozzarella cheese, grated or sliced thin
- 8 slider buns
- olive oil for misting
- 1 tablespoon sesame seeds
- Olive Mix
- ¼ cup sliced black olives
- ½ cup sliced green olives with pimentos
- ¼ cup chopped kalamata olives
- 1 teaspoon red wine vinegar
- ¼ teaspoon basil
- ⅛ teaspoon garlic powder

Directions:

1. In a small bowl, stir together all the Olive Mix ingredients.

2. Divide the meats and cheese into 8 equal portions. To assemble sliders, stack in this order: bottom bun, ham, pastrami, 2 tablespoons olive mix, cheese, top bun.

3. Mist tops of sliders lightly with oil. Sprinkle with sesame seeds.

4. Cooking 4 at a time, place sliders in air fryer basket and cook at 360°F for 7 minutes to melt cheese and heat through.

Herbed Cheese Brittle

Servings: 4

Cooking Time: 5 Minutes

Ingredients:

- ½ cup shredded Parmesan cheese
- ½ cup shredded white cheddar cheese
- 1 tablespoon fresh chopped rosemary
- 1 teaspoon garlic powder
- 1 large egg white

Directions:

1. Preheat the air fryer to 400°F.

2. In a large bowl, mix the cheeses, rosemary, and garlic powder. Mix in the egg white. Then pour the batter into a 7-inch pan (or an air-fryer-compatible pan). Place the pan in the air fryer basket and cook for 4 to 5 minutes, or until the cheese is melted and slightly browned.

3. Remove the pan from the air fryer, and let it cool for 2 minutes. Invert the pan before the cheese brittle completely cools but is semi-hardened to allow it to easily slide out of the pan.

4. Let the pan cool another 5 minutes. Break into pieces and serve.

Bacon Candy

Servings: 6

Cooking Time: 6 Minutes

Ingredients:

➤ 1½ tablespoons Honey

➤ 1 teaspoon White wine vinegar

➤ 3 Extra thick–cut bacon strips, halved widthwise (gluten-free, if a concern)

➤ ½ teaspoon Ground black pepper

Directions:

1. Preheat the air fryer to 350°F .

2. Whisk the honey and vinegar in a small bowl until incorporated.

3. When the machine is at temperature, remove the basket. Lay the bacon strip halves in the basket in one layer. Brush the tops with the honey mixture; sprinkle each bacon strip evenly with black pepper.

4. Return the basket to the machine and air-fry undisturbed for 6 minutes, or until the bacon is crunchy. Or a little less time if you prefer bacon that's still pliable, an extra minute if you want the bacon super crunchy. Take care that the honey coating doesn't burn. Remove the basket from the machine and set aside for 5 minutes. Use kitchen tongs to transfer the bacon strips to a serving plate.

Poultry Recipes

Chicken Nuggets

Servings: 20

Cooking Time: 14 Minutes Per Batch

Ingredients:

- ➢ 1 pound boneless, skinless chicken thighs, cut into 1-inch chunks
- ➢ ¾ teaspoon salt
- ➢ ½ teaspoon black pepper
- ➢ ½ teaspoon garlic powder
- ➢ ½ teaspoon onion powder
- ➢ ½ cup flour
- ➢ 2 eggs, beaten
- ➢ ½ cup panko breadcrumbs
- ➢ 3 tablespoons plain breadcrumbs
- ➢ oil for misting or cooking spray

Directions:

1. In the bowl of a food processor, combine chicken, ½ teaspoon salt, pepper, garlic powder, and onion powder. Process in short pulses until chicken is very finely chopped and well blended.

2. Place flour in one shallow dish and beaten eggs in another. In a third dish or plastic bag, mix together the panko crumbs, plain breadcrumbs, and ¼ teaspoon salt.

3. Shape chicken mixture into small nuggets. Dip nuggets in flour, then eggs, then panko crumb mixture.

4. Spray nuggets on both sides with oil or cooking spray and place in air fryer basket in a single layer, close but not overlapping.

5. Cook at 360°F for 10minutes. Spray with oil and cook 4 minutes, until chicken is done and coating is golden brown.

6. Repeat step 5 to cook remaining nuggets.

Turkey-hummus Wraps

Servings: 4

Cooking Time: 7 Minutes Per Batch

Ingredients:

- ➢ 4 large whole wheat wraps
- ➢ ½ cup hummus
- ➢ 16 thin slices deli turkey
- ➢ 8 slices provolone cheese
- ➢ 1 cup fresh baby spinach (or more to taste)

Directions:

1. To assemble, place 2 tablespoons of hummus on each wrap and spread to within about a half inch from edges. Top with 4 slices of turkey and 2 slices of provolone. Finish with ¼ cup of baby spinach—or pile on as much as you like.

2. Roll up each wrap. You don't need to fold or seal the ends.

3. Place 2 wraps in air fryer basket, seam side down.

4. Cook at 360°F for 4minutes to warm filling and melt cheese. If you like, you can continue cooking for 3 more minutes, until the wrap is slightly crispy.

5. Repeat step 4 to cook remaining wraps.

Southern-fried Chicken Livers

Servings: 4

Cooking Time: 12 Minutes

Ingredients:

- 2 eggs
- 2 tablespoons water
- ¾ cup flour
- 1½ cups panko breadcrumbs
- ½ cup plain breadcrumbs
- 1 teaspoon salt
- ½ teaspoon black pepper
- 20 ounces chicken livers, salted to taste
- oil for misting or cooking spray

Directions:

1. Beat together eggs and water in a shallow dish. Place the flour in a separate shallow dish.

2. In the bowl of a food processor, combine the panko, plain breadcrumbs, salt, and pepper. Process until well mixed and panko crumbs are finely crushed. Place crumbs in a third shallow dish.

3. Dip livers in flour, then egg wash, and then roll in panko mixture to coat well with crumbs.

4. Spray both sides of livers with oil or cooking spray. Cooking in two batches, place livers in air fryer basket in single layer.

5. Cook at 390°F for 7minutes. Spray livers, turn over, and spray again. Cook for 5 more minutes, until done inside and coating is golden brown.

6. Repeat to cook remaining livers.

Chicken Souvlaki Gyros

Servings: 4

Cooking Time: 18 Minutes

Ingredients:

- ¼ cup extra-virgin olive oil
- 1 clove garlic, crushed
- 1 tablespoon Italian seasoning
- ½ teaspoon paprika
- ½ lemon, sliced
- ¼ teaspoon salt
- 1 pound boneless, skinless chicken breasts
- 4 whole-grain pita breads
- 1 cup shredded lettuce
- ½ cup chopped tomatoes
- ¼ cup chopped red onion
- ¼ cup cucumber yogurt sauce

Directions:

1. In a large resealable plastic bag, combine the olive oil, garlic, Italian seasoning, paprika, lemon, and salt. Add the chicken to the bag and secure shut. Vigorously shake until all the ingredients are combined. Set in the fridge for 2 hours to marinate.

2. When ready to cook, preheat the air fryer to 360°F.

3. Liberally spray the air fryer basket with olive oil mist. Remove the chicken from the bag and discard the leftover marinade. Place the chicken into the air fryer basket, allowing enough room between the chicken breasts to flip.

4. Cook for 10 minutes, flip, and cook another 8 minutes.

5. Remove the chicken from the air fryer basket when it has cooked (or the internal temperature of the chicken reaches 165°F). Let rest 5 minutes. Then thinly slice the chicken into strips.

6. Assemble the gyros by placing the pita bread on a flat surface and topping with chicken, lettuce, tomatoes, onion, and a drizzle of yogurt sauce.

7. Serve warm.

Buffalo Egg Rolls

Servings: 8   Cooking Time: 9 Minutes Per Batch

Ingredients:

- 1 teaspoon water
- 1 tablespoon cornstarch
- 1 egg
- 2½ cups cooked chicken, diced or shredded (see opposite page)
- ⅓ cup chopped green onion
- ⅓ cup diced celery
- ⅓ cup buffalo wing sauce
- 8 egg roll wraps
- oil for misting or cooking spray
- Blue Cheese Dip
- 3 ounces cream cheese, softened
- ⅓ cup blue cheese, crumbled
- 1 teaspoon Worcestershire sauce
- ¼ teaspoon garlic powder
- ¼ cup buttermilk (or sour cream)

Directions:

1. Mix water and cornstarch in a small bowl until dissolved. Add egg, beat well, and set aside.
2. In a medium size bowl, mix together chicken, green onion, celery, and buffalo wing sauce.
3. Divide chicken mixture evenly among 8 egg roll wraps, spooning ½ inch from one edge.
4. Moisten all edges of each wrap with beaten egg wash.
5. Fold the short ends over filling, then roll up tightly and press to seal edges.
6. Brush outside of wraps with egg wash, then spritz with oil or cooking spray.
7. Place 4 egg rolls in air fryer basket.
8. Cook at 390°F for 9minutes or until outside is brown and crispy.
9. While the rolls are cooking, prepare the Blue Cheese Dip. With a fork, mash together cream cheese and blue cheese.
10. Stir in remaining ingredients.
11. Dip should be just thick enough to slightly cling to egg rolls. If too thick, stir in buttermilk or milk 1 tablespoon at a time until you reach the desired consistency.
12. Cook remaining 4 egg rolls as in steps 7 and 8.
13. Serve while hot with Blue Cheese Dip, more buffalo wing sauce, or both.

Chicken Rochambeau

Servings: 4   Cooking Time: 20 Minutes

Ingredients:

- 1 tablespoon butter
- 4 chicken tenders, cut in half crosswise
- salt and pepper
- ¼ cup flour
- oil for misting
- 4 slices ham, ¼- to ⅜-inches thick and large enough to cover an English muffin
- 2 English muffins, split

- Sauce
- 2 tablespoons butter
- ½ cup chopped green onions
- ½ cup chopped mushrooms
- 2 tablespoons flour
- 1 cup chicken broth
- ¼ teaspoon garlic powder
- 1½ teaspoons Worcestershire sauce

Directions:

1. Place 1 tablespoon of butter in air fryer baking pan and cook at 390°F for 2minutes to melt.

2. Sprinkle chicken tenders with salt and pepper to taste, then roll in the ¼ cup of flour.

3. Place chicken in baking pan, turning pieces to coat with melted butter.

4. Cook at 390°F for 5minutes. Turn chicken pieces over, and spray tops lightly with olive oil. Cook 5minutes longer or until juices run clear. The chicken will not brown.

5. While chicken is cooking, make the sauce: In a medium saucepan, melt the 2 tablespoons of butter.

6. Add onions and mushrooms and sauté until tender, about 3minutes.

7. Stir in the flour. Gradually add broth, stirring constantly until you have a smooth gravy.

8. Add garlic powder and Worcestershire sauce and simmer on low heat until sauce thickens, about 5minutes.

9. When chicken is cooked, remove baking pan from air fryer and set aside.

10. Place ham slices directly into air fryer basket and cook at 390°F for 5minutes or until hot and beginning to sizzle a little. Remove and set aside on top of the chicken for now.

11. Place the English muffin halves in air fryer basket and cook at 390°F for 1 minute.

12. Open air fryer and place a ham slice on top of each English muffin half. Stack 2 pieces of chicken on top of each ham slice. Cook at 390°F for 1 to 2minutes to heat through.

13. Place each English muffin stack on a serving plate and top with plenty of sauce.

Chicken Chunks

Servings: 4

Cooking Time: 10 Minutes

Ingredients:

➤ 1 pound chicken tenders cut in large chunks, about 1½ inches

➤ salt and pepper

➤ ½ cup cornstarch

➤ 2 eggs, beaten

➤ 1 cup panko breadcrumbs

➤ oil for misting or cooking spray

Directions:

1. Season chicken chunks to your liking with salt and pepper.

2. Dip chicken chunks in cornstarch. Then dip in egg and shake off excess. Then roll in panko crumbs to coat well.

3. Spray all sides of chicken chunks with oil or cooking spray.

4. Place chicken in air fryer basket in single layer and cook at 390°F for 5minutes. Spray with oil, turn chunks over, and spray other side.

5. Cook for an additional 5minutes or until chicken juices run clear and outside is golden brown.

6. Repeat steps 4 and 5 to cook remaining chicken.

Southern-style Chicken Legs

Servings: 6

Cooking Time: 20 Minutes

Ingredients:

- ➢ 2 cups buttermilk
- ➢ 1 tablespoon hot sauce
- ➢ 12 chicken legs
- ➢ ½ teaspoon salt
- ➢ ½ teaspoon pepper
- ➢ 1 teaspoon paprika
- ➢ ½ teaspoon onion powder
- ➢ 1 teaspoon garlic powder
- ➢ 1 cup all-purpose flour

Directions:

1. In an airtight container, place the buttermilk, hot sauce, and chicken legs and refrigerate for 4 to 8 hours.

2. In a medium bowl, whisk together the salt, pepper, paprika, onion powder, garlic powder, and flour. Drain the chicken legs from the buttermilk and dip the chicken legs into the flour mixture, stirring to coat well.

3. Preheat the air fryer to 390°F.

4. Place the chicken legs in the air fryer basket and spray with cooking spray. Cook for 10 minutes, turn the chicken legs over, and cook for another 8 to 10 minutes. Check for an internal temperature of 165°F.

Teriyaki Chicken Legs

Servings: 2

Cooking Time: 20 Minutes

Ingredients:

- ➢ 4 tablespoons teriyaki sauce
- ➢ 1 tablespoon orange juice
- ➢ 1 teaspoon smoked paprika
- ➢ 4 chicken legs
- ➢ cooking spray

Directions:

1. Mix together the teriyaki sauce, orange juice, and smoked paprika. Brush on all sides of chicken legs.

2. Spray air fryer basket with nonstick cooking spray and place chicken in basket.

3. Cook at 360°F for 6minutes. Turn and baste with sauce. Cook for 6 moreminutes, turn and baste.

Cook for 8 minutes more, until juices run clear when chicken is pierced with a fork.

Thai Chicken Drumsticks

Servings: 4

Cooking Time: 20 Minutes

Ingredients:

- 2 tablespoons soy sauce
- ¼ cup rice wine vinegar
- 2 tablespoons chili garlic sauce
- 2 tablespoons sesame oil
- 1 teaspoon minced fresh ginger
- 2 teaspoons sugar
- ½ teaspoon ground coriander
- juice of 1 lime
- 8 chicken drumsticks (about 2½ pounds)
- ¼ cup chopped peanuts
- chopped fresh cilantro
- lime wedges

Directions:

1. Combine the soy sauce, rice wine vinegar, chili sauce, sesame oil, ginger, sugar, coriander and lime juice in a large bowl and mix together. Add the chicken drumsticks and marinate for 30 minutes.

2. Preheat the air fryer to 370°F.

3. Place the chicken in the air fryer basket. It's ok if the ends of the drumsticks overlap a little. Spoon half of the marinade over the chicken, and reserve the other half.

4. Air-fry for 10 minutes. Turn the chicken over and pour the rest of the marinade over the chicken. Air-fry for an additional 10 minutes.

5. Transfer the chicken to a plate to rest and cool to an edible temperature. Pour the marinade from the bottom of the air fryer into a small saucepan and bring it to a simmer over medium-high heat. Simmer the liquid for 2 minutes so that it thickens enough to coat the back of a spoon.

6. Transfer the chicken to a serving platter, pour the sauce over the chicken and sprinkle the chopped peanuts on top. Garnish with chopped cilantro and lime wedges.

Southwest Gluten-free Turkey Meatloaf

Servings: 8

Cooking Time: 35 Minutes

Ingredients:

- 1 pound lean ground turkey
- ¼ cup corn grits
- ¼ cup diced onion
- 1 teaspoon minced garlic
- ½ teaspoon black pepper
- ½ teaspoon salt
- 1 large egg
- ½ cup ketchup
- 4 teaspoons chipotle hot sauce
- ⅓ cup shredded cheddar cheese

Directions:

1. Preheat the air fryer to 350°F.
2. In a large bowl, mix together the ground turkey, corn grits, onion, garlic, black pepper, and salt.
3. In a small bowl, whisk the egg. Add the egg to the turkey mixture and combine.
4. In a small bowl, mix the ketchup and hot sauce. Set aside.
5. Liberally spray a 9-x-4-inch loaf pan with olive oil spray. Depending on the size of your air fryer, you may need to use 2 or 3 mini loaf pans.
6. Spoon the ground turkey mixture into the loaf pan and evenly top with half of the ketchup mixture. Cover with foil and place the meatloaf into the air fryer. Cook for 30 minutes; remove the foil and discard. Check the internal temperature (it should be nearing 165°F).
7. Coat the top of the meatloaf with the remaining ketchup mixture, and sprinkle the cheese over the top. Place the meatloaf back in the air fryer for the remaining 5 minutes (or until the internal temperature reaches 165°F).
8. Remove from the oven and let cool 5 minutes before serving. Serve warm with desired sides.

Gluten-free Nutty Chicken Fingers

Servings: 4

Cooking Time: 10 Minutes

Ingredients:

- ½ cup gluten-free flour
- ½ teaspoon garlic powder
- ¼ teaspoon onion powder
- ¼ teaspoon black pepper
- ¼ teaspoon salt
- 1 cup walnuts, pulsed into coarse flour
- ½ cup gluten-free breadcrumbs
- 2 large eggs
- 1 pound boneless, skinless chicken tenders

Directions:

1. Preheat the air fryer to 400°F.
2. In a medium bowl, mix the flour, garlic, onion, pepper, and salt. Set aside.
3. In a separate bowl, mix the walnut flour and breadcrumbs.
4. In a third bowl, whisk the eggs.
5. Liberally spray the air fryer basket with olive oil spray.
6. Pat the chicken tenders dry with a paper towel. Dredge the tenders one at a time in the flour, then dip them in the egg, and toss them in the breadcrumb coating. Repeat until all tenders are coated.
7. Set each tender in the air fryer, leaving room on each side of the tender to allow for flipping.
8. When the basket is full, cook 5 minutes, flip, and cook another 5 minutes. Check the internal temperature after cooking completes; it should read 165°F. If it does not, cook another 2 to 4 minutes.
9. Remove the tenders and let cool 5 minutes before serving. Repeat until all the tenders are cooked.

Mediterranean Stuffed Chicken Breasts

Servings: 4

Cooking Time: 24 Minutes

Ingredients:

- ➢ 4 boneless, skinless chicken breasts
- ➢ ½ teaspoon salt
- ➢ ½ teaspoon black pepper
- ➢ ½ teaspoon garlic powder
- ➢ ½ teaspoon paprika
- ➢ ½ cup canned artichoke hearts, chopped
- ➢ 4 ounces cream cheese
- ➢ ¼ cup grated Parmesan cheese

Directions:

1. Pat the chicken breasts with a paper towel. Using a sharp knife, cut a pouch in the side of each chicken breast for filling.

2. In a small bowl, mix the salt, pepper, garlic powder, and paprika. Season the chicken breasts with this mixture.

3. In a medium bowl, mix together the artichokes, cream cheese, and grated Parmesan cheese. Divide the filling between the 4 breasts, stuffing it inside the pouches. Use toothpicks to close the pouches and secure the filling.

4. Preheat the air fryer to 360°F.

5. Spray the air fryer basket liberally with cooking spray, add the stuffed chicken breasts to the basket, and spray liberally with cooking spray again. Cook for 14 minutes, carefully turn over the chicken breasts, and cook another 10 minutes. Check the temperature at 20 minutes cooking. Chicken breasts are fully cooked when the center measures 165°F. Cook in batches, if needed.

Desserts And Sweets

Dark Chocolate Peanut Butter S'mores

Servings: 4

Cooking Time: 6 Minutes

Ingredients:

➤ 4 graham cracker sheets

➤ 4 marshmallows

➤ 4 teaspoons chunky peanut butter

➤ 4 ounces dark chocolate

➤ ½ teaspoon ground cinnamon

Directions:

1. Preheat the air fryer to 390°F. Break the graham crackers in half so you have 8 pieces.

2. Place 4 pieces of graham cracker on the bottom of the air fryer. Top each with one of the marshmallows and bake for 6 or 7 minutes, or until the marshmallows have a golden brown center.

3. While cooking, slather each of the remaining graham crackers with 1 teaspoon peanut butter.

4. When baking completes, carefully remove each of the graham crackers, add 1 ounce of dark chocolate on top of the marshmallow, and lightly sprinkle with cinnamon. Top with the remaining peanut butter graham cracker to make the sandwich. Serve immediately.

Gingerbread

Servings: 6

Cooking Time: 20 Minutes

Ingredients:

- ➢ cooking spray
- ➢ 1 cup flour
- ➢ 2 tablespoons sugar
- ➢ ¾ teaspoon ground ginger
- ➢ ¼ teaspoon cinnamon
- ➢ 1 teaspoon baking powder
- ➢ ½ teaspoon baking soda
- ➢ ⅛ teaspoon salt
- ➢ 1 egg
- ➢ ¼ cup molasses
- ➢ ½ cup buttermilk
- ➢ 2 tablespoons oil
- ➢ 1 teaspoon pure vanilla extract

Directions:

1. Preheat air fryer to 330°F.
2. Spray 6 x 6-inch baking dish lightly with cooking spray.
3. In a medium bowl, mix together all the dry ingredients.
4. In a separate bowl, beat the egg. Add molasses, buttermilk, oil, and vanilla and stir until well mixed.
5. Pour liquid mixture into dry ingredients and stir until well blended.
6. Pour batter into baking dish and cook at 330°F for 20minutes or until toothpick inserted in center of loaf comes out clean.

Sea-salted Caramel Cookie Cups

Servings: 12

Cooking Time: 12 Minutes

Ingredients:

- ⅓ cup butter
- ¼ cup brown sugar
- 1 teaspoon vanilla extract
- 1 large egg
- 1 cup all-purpose flour
- ½ cup old-fashioned oats
- ½ teaspoon baking soda
- ¼ teaspoon salt
- ⅓ cup sea-salted caramel chips

Directions:

1. Preheat the air fryer to 300°F.

2. In a large bowl, cream the butter with the brown sugar and vanilla. Whisk in the egg and set aside.

3. In a separate bowl, mix the flour, oats, baking soda, and salt. Then gently mix the dry ingredients into the wet. Fold in the caramel chips.

4. Divide the batter into 12 silicon muffin liners. Place the cookie cups into the air fryer basket and cook for 12 minutes or until a toothpick inserted in the center comes out clean.

5. Remove and let cool 5 minutes before serving.

Cheese Blintzes

Servings: 6

Cooking Time: 10 Minutes

Ingredients:

➢ 1½ 7½-ounce package(s) farmer cheese

➢ 3 tablespoons Regular or low-fat cream cheese (not fat-free)

➢ 3 tablespoons Granulated white sugar

➢ ¼ teaspoon Vanilla extract

➢ 6 Egg roll wrappers

➢ 3 tablespoons Butter, melted and cooled

Directions:

1. Preheat the air fryer to 375°F .

2. Use a flatware fork to mash the farmer cheese, cream cheese, sugar, and vanilla in a small bowl until smooth.

3. Set one egg roll wrapper on a clean, dry work surface. Place ¼ cup of the filling at the edge closest to you, leaving a ½-inch gap before the edge of the wrapper. Dip your clean finger in water and wet the edges of the wrapper. Fold the perpendicular sides over the filling, then roll the wrapper closed with the filling inside. Set it aside seam side down and continue filling the remainder of the wrappers.

4. Brush the wrappers on all sides with the melted butter. Be generous. Set them seam side down in the basket with as much space between them as possible. Air-fry undisturbed for 10 minutes, or until lightly browned.

5. Use a nonstick-safe spatula to transfer the blintzes to a wire rack. Cool for at least 5 minutes or up to 20 minutes before serving.

Bananas Foster Bread Pudding

Servings: 4

Cooking Time: 25 Minutes

Ingredients:

- ½ cup brown sugar
- 3 eggs
- ¾ cup half and half
- 1 teaspoon pure vanilla extract
- 6 cups cubed Kings Hawaiian bread (½-inch cubes), ½ pound
- 2 bananas, sliced
- 1 cup caramel sauce, plus more for serving

Directions:

1. Preheat the air fryer to 350°F.

2. Combine the brown sugar, eggs, half and half and vanilla extract in a large bowl, whisking until the sugar has dissolved and the mixture is smooth. Stir in the cubed bread and toss to coat all the cubes evenly. Let the bread sit for 10 minutes to absorb the liquid.

3. Mix the sliced bananas and caramel sauce together in a separate bowl.

4. Fill the bottom of 4 (8-ounce) greased ramekins with half the bread cubes. Divide the caramel and bananas between the ramekins, spooning them on top of the bread cubes. Top with the remaining bread cubes and wrap each ramekin with aluminum foil, tenting the foil at the top to leave some room for the bread to puff up during the cooking process.

5. Air-fry two bread puddings at a time for 25 minutes. Let the puddings cool a little and serve warm with additional caramel sauce drizzled on top. A scoop of vanilla ice cream would be nice too and in keeping with our Bananas Foster theme!

Peach Cobbler

Servings: 4

Cooking Time: 12 Minutes

Ingredients:

- ➢ 16 ounces frozen peaches, thawed, with juice (do not drain)
- ➢ 6 tablespoons sugar
- ➢ 1 tablespoon cornstarch
- ➢ 1 tablespoon water
- ➢ Crust
- ➢ ½ cup flour
- ➢ ¼ teaspoon salt
- ➢ 3 tablespoons butter
- ➢ 1½ tablespoons cold water
- ➢ ¼ teaspoon sugar

Directions:

1. Place peaches, including juice, and sugar in air fryer baking pan. Stir to mix well.
2. In a small cup, dissolve cornstarch in the water. Stir into peaches.
3. In a medium bowl, combine the flour and salt. Cut in butter using knives or a pastry blender. Stir in the cold water to make a stiff dough.
4. On a floured board or wax paper, pat dough into a square or circle slightly smaller than your air fryer baking pan. Cut diagonally into 4 pieces.
5. Place dough pieces on top of peaches, leaving a tiny bit of space between the edges. Sprinkle very lightly with sugar, no more than about ¼ teaspoon.
6. Cook at 360°F for 12 minutes, until fruit bubbles and crust browns.

Giant Oatmeal–peanut Butter Cookie

Servings: 4

Cooking Time: 18 Minutes

Ingredients:

- 1 cup Rolled oats (not quick-cooking or steel-cut oats)
- ½ cup All-purpose flour
- ½ teaspoon Ground cinnamon
- ½ teaspoon Baking soda
- ⅓ cup Packed light brown sugar
- ¼ cup Solid vegetable shortening
- 2 tablespoons Natural-style creamy peanut butter
- 3 tablespoons Granulated white sugar
- 2 tablespoons (or 1 small egg, well beaten) Pasteurized egg substitute, such as Egg Beaters
- ⅓ cup Roasted, salted peanuts, chopped
- Baking spray

Directions:

1. Preheat the air fryer to 350°F .
2. Stir the oats, flour, cinnamon, and baking soda in a bowl until well combined.
3. Using an electric hand mixer at medium speed, beat the brown sugar, shortening, peanut butter, granulated white sugar, and egg substitute or egg (as applicable) until smooth and creamy, about 3 minutes, scraping down the inside of the bowl occasionally.
4. Scrape down and remove the beaters. Fold in the flour mixture and peanuts with a rubber spatula just until all the flour is moistened and the peanut bits are evenly distributed in the dough.
5. For a small air fryer, coat the inside of a 6-inch round cake pan with baking spray. For a medium air fryer, coat the inside of a 7-inch round cake pan with baking spray. And for a large air fryer, coat the inside of an 8-inch round cake pan with baking spray. Scrape and gently press the dough into the prepared pan, spreading it into an even layer to the perimeter.
6. Set the pan in the basket and air-fry undisturbed for 18 minutes, or until well browned.
7. Transfer the pan to a wire rack and cool for 15 minutes. Loosen the cookie from the perimeter with a spatula, then invert the pan onto a cutting board and let the cookie come free. Remove the pan and reinvert the cookie onto the wire rack. Cool for 5 minutes more before slicing into wedges to serve.

Almond-roasted Pears

Servings: 4

Cooking Time: 15 Minutes

Ingredients:

- ➤ Yogurt Topping
- ➤ 1 container vanilla Greek yogurt (5–6 ounces)
- ➤ ¼ teaspoon almond flavoring
- ➤ 2 whole pears
- ➤ ¼ cup crushed Biscoff cookies (approx. 4 cookies)
- ➤ 1 tablespoon sliced almonds
- ➤ 1 tablespoon butter

Directions:

1. Stir almond flavoring into yogurt and set aside while preparing pears.
2. Halve each pear and spoon out the core.
3. Place pear halves in air fryer basket.
4. Stir together the cookie crumbs and almonds. Place a quarter of this mixture into the hollow of each pear half.
5. Cut butter into 4 pieces and place one piece on top of crumb mixture in each pear.
6. Cook at 360°F for 15 minutes or until pears have cooked through but are still slightly firm.
7. Serve pears warm with a dollop of yogurt topping.

Sugared Pizza Dough Dippers With Raspberry Cream Cheese Dip

Servings: 10   Cooking Time: 8 Minutes

Ingredients:

- 1 pound pizza dough*
- ½ cup butter, melted
- ¾ to 1 cup sugar
- Raspberry Cream Cheese Dip
- 4 ounces cream cheese, softened

- 2 tablespoons powdered sugar
- ½ teaspoon almond extract or almond paste
- 1½ tablespoons milk
- ¼ cup raspberry preserves
- fresh raspberries

Directions:

1. Cut the ingredients in half or save half of the dough for another recipe.

2. When you're ready to make your sugared dough dippers, remove your pizza dough from the refrigerator at least 1 hour prior to baking and let it sit on the counter, covered gently with plastic wrap.

3. Roll the dough into two 15-inch logs. Cut each log into 20 slices and roll each slice so that it is 3- to 3½-inches long. Cut each slice in half and twist the dough halves together 3 to 4 times. Place the twisted dough on a cookie sheet, brush with melted butter and sprinkle sugar over the dough twists.

4. Preheat the air fryer to 350°F.

5. Brush the bottom of the air fryer basket with a little melted butter. Air-fry the dough twists in batches. Place 8 to 12 (depending on the size of your air fryer) in the air fryer basket.

6. Air-fry for 6 minutes. Turn the dough strips over and brush the other side with butter. Air-fry for an additional 2 minutes.

7. While the dough twists are cooking, make the cream cheese and raspberry dip. Whip the cream cheese with a hand mixer until fluffy. Add the powdered sugar, almond extract and milk, and beat until smooth. Fold in the raspberry preserves and transfer to a serving dish.

8. As the batches of dough twists are complete, place them into a shallow dish. Brush with more melted butter and generously coat with sugar, shaking the dish to cover both sides. Serve the sugared dough dippers warm with the raspberry cream cheese dip on the side. Garnish with fresh raspberries.

Coconut Crusted Bananas With Pineapple Sauce

Servings: 4

Cooking Time: 5 Minutes

Ingredients:

➢ Pineapple Sauce

➢ 1½ cups puréed fresh pineapple

➢ 2 tablespoons sugar

➢ juice of 1 lemon

➢ ¼ teaspoon ground cinnamon

➢ 3 firm bananas

➢ ¼ cup sweetened condensed milk

➢ 1¼ cups shredded coconut

➢ ⅓ cup crushed graham crackers (crumbs)*

➢ vegetable or canola oil, in a spray bottle

➢ vanilla frozen yogurt or ice cream

Directions:

1. Make the pineapple sauce by combining the pineapple, sugar, lemon juice and cinnamon in a saucepan. Simmer the mixture on the stovetop for 20 minutes, and then set it aside.

2. Slice the bananas diagonally into ½-inch thick slices and place them in a bowl. Pour the sweetened condensed milk into the bowl and toss the bananas gently to coat. Combine the coconut and graham cracker crumbs together in a shallow dish. Remove the banana slices from the condensed milk and let any excess milk drip off. Dip the banana slices in the coconut and crumb mixture to coat both sides. Spray the coated slices with oil.

3. Preheat the air fryer to 400°F.

4. Grease the bottom of the air fryer basket with a little oil. Air-fry the bananas in batches at 400°F for 5 minutes, turning them over halfway through the cooking time. Air-fry until the bananas are golden brown on both sides.

5. Serve warm over vanilla frozen yogurt with some of the pineapple sauce spooned over top.

Apple Crisp

Servings: 4

Cooking Time: 16 Minutes

Ingredients:

- ➤ Filling
- ➤ 3 Granny Smith apples, thinly sliced (about 4 cups)
- ➤ ¼ teaspoon ground cinnamon
- ➤ ⅛ teaspoon salt
- ➤ 1½ teaspoons lemon juice
- ➤ 2 tablespoons honey
- ➤ 1 tablespoon brown sugar
- ➤ cooking spray
- ➤ Crumb Topping
- ➤ 2 tablespoons oats
- ➤ 2 tablespoons oat bran
- ➤ 2 tablespoons cooked quinoa
- ➤ 2 tablespoons chopped walnuts
- ➤ 2 tablespoons brown sugar
- ➤ 2 teaspoons coconut oil

Directions:

1. Combine all filling ingredients and stir well so that apples are evenly coated.

2. Spray air fryer baking pan with nonstick cooking spray and spoon in the apple mixture.

3. Cook at 360°F for 5minutes. Stir well, scooping up from the bottom to mix apples and sauce.

4. At this point, the apples should be crisp-tender. Continue cooking in 3-minute intervals until apples are as soft as you like.

5. While apples are cooking, combine all topping ingredients in a small bowl. Stir until coconut oil mixes in well and distributes evenly. If your coconut oil is cold, it may be easier to mix in by hand.

6. When apples are cooked to your liking, sprinkle crumb mixture on top. Cook at 360°F for 8 minutes or until crumb topping is golden brown and crispy.

Honey-pecan Yogurt Cake

Servings: 6   Cooking Time: 18-24 Minutes

Ingredients:

- 1 cup plus 3½ tablespoons All-purpose flour
- ¼ teaspoon Baking powder
- ¼ teaspoon Baking soda
- ¼ teaspoon Table salt
- 5 tablespoons Plain full-fat, low-fat, or fat-free Greek yogurt

- 5 tablespoons Honey
- 5 tablespoons Pasteurized egg substitute, such as Egg Beaters
- 2 teaspoons Vanilla extract
- ⅔ cup Chopped pecans
- Baking spray (see here)

Directions:

1. Preheat the air fryer to 325°F (or 330°F, if the closest setting).

2. Mix the flour, baking powder, baking soda, and salt in a small bowl until well combined.

3. Using an electric hand mixer at medium speed , beat the yogurt, honey, egg substitute or egg, and vanilla in a medium bowl until smooth, about 2 minutes, scraping down the inside of the bowl once or twice.

4. Turn off the mixer; scrape down and remove the beaters. Fold in the flour mixture with a rubber spatula, just until all of the flour has been moistened. Fold in the pecans until they are evenly distributed in the mixture.

5. Use the baking spray to generously coat the inside of a 6-inch round cake pan for a small batch, a 7-inch round cake pan for a medium batch, or an 8-inch round cake pan for a large batch. Scrape and spread the batter into the pan, smoothing the batter out to an even layer.

6. Set the pan in the basket and air-fry for 18 minutes for a 6-inch layer, 22 minutes for a 7-inch layer, or 24 minutes for an 8-inch layer, or until a toothpick or cake tester inserted into the center of the cake comes out clean. Start checking it at the 15-minute mark to know where you are.

7. Use hot pads or silicone baking mitts to transfer the cake pan to a wire rack. Cool for 5 minutes. To unmold, set a cutting board over the baking pan and invert both the board and the pan. Lift the still-warm pan off the cake layer. Set the wire rack on top of that layer and invert all of it with the cutting board so that the cake layer is now right side up on the wire rack. Remove the cutting board and continue cooling the cake for at least 10 minutes or to room temperature, about 30 minutes, before slicing into wedges.

Cherry Hand Pies

Servings: 8

Cooking Time: 8 Minutes

Ingredients:

➢ 4 cups frozen or canned pitted tart cherries (if using canned, drain and pat dry)

➢ 2 teaspoons lemon juice

➢ ½ cup sugar

➢ ¼ cup cornstarch

➢ 1 teaspoon vanilla extract

➢ 1 Basic Pie Dough (see the preceding recipe) or store-bought pie dough

Directions:

1. In a medium saucepan, place the cherries and lemon juice and cook over medium heat for 10 minutes, or until the cherries begin to break down.

2. In a small bowl, stir together the sugar and cornstarch. Pour the sugar mixture into the cherries, stirring constantly. Cook the cherry mixture over low heat for 2 to 3 minutes, or until thickened. Remove from the heat and stir in the vanilla extract. Allow the cherry mixture to cool to room temperature, about 30 minutes.

3. Meanwhile, bring the pie dough to room temperature. Divide the dough into 8 equal pieces. Roll out the dough to ¼-inch thickness in circles. Place ¼ cup filling in the center of each rolled dough. Fold the dough to create a half-circle. Using a fork, press around the edges to seal the hand pies. Pierce the top of the pie with a fork for steam release while cooking. Continue until 8 hand pies are formed.

4. Preheat the air fryer to 350°F.

5. Place a single layer of hand pies in the air fryer basket and spray with cooking spray. Cook for 8 to 10 minutes or until golden brown and cooked through.

Vegetarians Recipes

Cauliflower Steaks Gratin

Servings: 2
Cooking Time: 13 Minutes

Ingredients:

➢ 1 head cauliflower
➢ 1 tablespoon olive oil
➢ salt and freshly ground black pepper
➢ ½ teaspoon chopped fresh thyme leaves
➢ 3 tablespoons grated Parmigiano-Reggiano cheese
➢ 2 tablespoons panko breadcrumbs

Directions:

1. Preheat the air-fryer to 370°F.

2. Cut two steaks out of the center of the cauliflower. To do this, cut the cauliflower in half and then cut one slice about 1-inch thick off each half. The rest of the cauliflower will fall apart into florets, which you can roast on their own or save for another meal.

3. Brush both sides of the cauliflower steaks with olive oil and season with salt, freshly ground black pepper and fresh thyme. Place the cauliflower steaks into the air fryer basket and air-fry for 6 minutes. Turn the steaks over and air-fry for another 4 minutes. Combine the Parmesan cheese and panko breadcrumbs and sprinkle the mixture over the tops of both steaks and air-fry for another 3 minutes until the cheese has melted and the breadcrumbs have browned. Serve this with some sautéed bitter greens and air-fried blistered tomatoes.

Spicy Sesame Tempeh Slaw With Peanut Dressing

Servings: 2   Cooking Time: 8 Minutes

Ingredients:

- 2 cups hot water
- 1 teaspoon salt
- 8 ounces tempeh, sliced into 1-inch-long pieces
- 2 tablespoons low-sodium soy sauce
- 2 tablespoons rice vinegar
- 1 tablespoon filtered water
- 2 teaspoons sesame oil
- ½ teaspoon fresh ginger

- 1 clove garlic, minced
- ¼ teaspoon black pepper
- ½ jalapeño, sliced
- 4 cups cabbage slaw
- 4 tablespoons Peanut Dressing (see the following recipe)
- 2 tablespoons fresh chopped cilantro
- 2 tablespoons chopped peanuts

Directions:

1. Mix the hot water with the salt and pour over the tempeh in a glass bowl. Stir and cover with a towel for 10 minutes.

2. Discard the water and leave the tempeh in the bowl.

3. In a medium bowl, mix the soy sauce, rice vinegar, filtered water, sesame oil, ginger, garlic, pepper, and jalapeño. Pour over the tempeh and cover with a towel. Place in the refrigerator to marinate for at least 2 hours.

4. Preheat the air fryer to 370°F. Remove the tempeh from the bowl and discard the remaining marinade.

5. Liberally spray the metal trivet that goes into the air fryer basket and place the tempeh on top of the trivet.

6. Cook for 4 minutes, flip, and cook another 4 minutes.

7. In a large bowl, mix the cabbage slaw with the Peanut Dressing and toss in the cilantro and chopped peanuts.

8. Portion onto 4 plates and place the cooked tempeh on top when cooking completes. Serve immediately.

Roasted Vegetable, Brown Rice And Black Bean Burrito

Servings: 2   Cooking Time: 20 Minutes

Ingredients:

- ½ zucchini, sliced ¼-inch thick
- ½ red onion, sliced
- 1 yellow bell pepper, sliced
- 2 teaspoons olive oil
- salt and freshly ground black pepper
- 2 burrito size flour tortillas
- 1 cup grated pepper jack cheese
- ½ cup cooked brown rice
- ½ cup canned black beans, drained and rinsed
- ¼ teaspoon ground cumin
- 1 tablespoon chopped fresh cilantro
- fresh salsa, guacamole and sour cream, for serving

Directions:

1. Preheat the air fryer to 400°F.

2. Toss the vegetables in a bowl with the olive oil, salt and freshly ground black pepper. Air-fry at 400°F for 12 to 15 minutes, shaking the basket a few times during the cooking process. The vegetables are done when they are cooked to your liking.

3. In the meantime, start building the burritos. Lay the tortillas out on the counter. Sprinkle half of the cheese in the center of the tortillas. Combine the rice, beans, cumin and cilantro in a bowl, season to taste with salt and freshly ground black pepper and then divide the mixture between the two tortillas. When the vegetables have finished cooking, transfer them to the two tortillas, placing the vegetables on top of the rice and beans. Sprinkle the remaining cheese on top and then roll the burritos up, tucking in the sides of the tortillas as you roll. Brush or spray the outside of the burritos with olive oil and transfer them to the air fryer.

4. Air-fry at 360°F for 8 minutes, turning them over when there are about 2 minutes left. The burritos will have slightly brown spots, but will still be pliable.

5. Serve with some fresh salsa, guacamole and sour cream.

Spinach And Cheese Calzone

Servings: 2

Cooking Time: 10 Minutes

Ingredients:

- ⅔ cup frozen chopped spinach, thawed
- 1 cup grated mozzarella cheese
- 1 cup ricotta cheese
- ½ teaspoon Italian seasoning
- ½ teaspoon salt
- freshly ground black pepper
- 1 store-bought or homemade pizza dough* (about 12 to 16 ounces)
- 2 tablespoons olive oil
- pizza or marinara sauce (optional)

Directions:

1. Drain and squeeze all the water out of the thawed spinach and set it aside. Mix the mozzarella cheese, ricotta cheese, Italian seasoning, salt and freshly ground black pepper together in a bowl. Stir in the chopped spinach.

2. Divide the dough in half. With floured hands or on a floured surface, stretch or roll one half of the dough into a 10-inch circle. Spread half of the cheese and spinach mixture on half of the dough, leaving about one inch of dough empty around the edge.

3. Fold the other half of the dough over the cheese mixture, almost to the edge of the bottom dough to form a half moon. Fold the bottom edge of dough up over the top edge and crimp the dough around the edges in order to make the crust and seal the calzone. Brush the dough with olive oil. Repeat with the second half of dough to make the second calzone.

4. Preheat the air fryer to 360°F.

5. Brush or spray the air fryer basket with olive oil. Air-fry the calzones one at a time for 10 minutes, flipping the calzone over half way through. Serve with warm pizza or marinara sauce if desired.

Rigatoni With Roasted Onions, Fennel, Spinach And Lemon Pepper Ricotta

Servings: 2

Cooking Time: 13 Minutes

Ingredients:

- 1 red onion, rough chopped into large chunks
- 2 teaspoons olive oil, divided
- 1 bulb fennel, sliced ¼-inch thick
- ¾ cup ricotta cheese
- 1½ teaspoons finely chopped lemon zest, plus more for garnish
- 1 teaspoon lemon juice
- salt and freshly ground black pepper
- 8 ounces (½ pound) dried rigatoni pasta
- 3 cups baby spinach leaves

Directions:

1. Bring a large stockpot of salted water to a boil on the stovetop and Preheat the air fryer to 400°F.

2. While the water is coming to a boil, toss the chopped onion in 1 teaspoon of olive oil and transfer to the air fryer basket. Air-fry at 400°F for 5 minutes. Toss the sliced fennel with 1 teaspoon of olive oil and add this to the air fryer basket with the onions. Continue to air-fry at 400°F for 8 minutes, shaking the basket a few times during the cooking process.

3. Combine the ricotta cheese, lemon zest and juice, ¼ teaspoon of salt and freshly ground black pepper in a bowl and stir until smooth.

4. Add the dried rigatoni to the boiling water and cook according to the package directions. When the pasta is cooked al dente, reserve one cup of the pasta water and drain the pasta into a colander.

5. Place the spinach in a serving bowl and immediately transfer the hot pasta to the bowl, wilting the spinach. Add the roasted onions and fennel and toss together. Add a little pasta water to the dish if it needs moistening. Then, dollop the lemon pepper ricotta cheese on top and nestle it into the hot pasta. Garnish with more lemon zest if desired.

Lentil Fritters

Servings: 9

Cooking Time: 12 Minutes

Ingredients:

- ➢ 1 cup cooked red lentils
- ➢ 1 cup riced cauliflower
- ➢ ½ medium zucchini, shredded (about 1 cup)
- ➢ ¼ cup finely chopped onion
- ➢ ¼ teaspoon salt
- ➢ ¼ teaspoon black pepper
- ➢ ½ teaspoon garlic powder
- ➢ ¼ teaspoon paprika
- ➢ 1 large egg
- ➢ ⅓ cup quinoa flour

Directions:

1. Preheat the air fryer to 370°F.

2. In a large bowl, mix the lentils, cauliflower, zucchini, onion, salt, pepper, garlic powder, and paprika. Mix in the egg and flour until a thick dough forms.

3. Using a large spoon, form the dough into 9 large fritters.

4. Liberally spray the air fryer basket with olive oil. Place the fritters into the basket, leaving space around each fritter so you can flip them.

5. Cook for 6 minutes, flip, and cook another 6 minutes.

6. Remove from the air fryer and repeat with the remaining fritters. Serve warm with desired sauce and sides.

Roasted Vegetable Stromboli

Servings: 2   Cooking Time: 29 Minutes

Ingredients:

- ½ onion, thinly sliced
- ½ red pepper, julienned
- ½ yellow pepper, julienned
- olive oil
- 1 small zucchini, thinly sliced
- 1 cup thinly sliced mushrooms
- 1½ cups chopped broccoli
- 1 teaspoon Italian seasoning
- salt and freshly ground black pepper

- ½ recipe of Blue Jean Chef Pizza dough (page 231) OR 1 (14-ounce) tube refrigerated pizza dough
- 2 cups grated mozzarella cheese
- ¼ cup grated Parmesan cheese
- ½ cup sliced black olives, optional
- dried oregano
- pizza or marinara sauce

Directions:

1. Preheat the air fryer to 400°F.
2. Toss the onions and peppers with a little olive oil and air-fry the vegetables for 7 minutes, shaking the basket once or twice while the vegetables cook. Add the zucchini, mushrooms, broccoli and Italian seasoning to the basket. Add a little more olive oil and season with salt and freshly ground black pepper. Air-fry for an additional 7 minutes, shaking the basket halfway through. Let the vegetables cool slightly while you roll out the pizza dough.
3. On a lightly floured surface, roll or press the pizza dough out into a 13-inch by 11-inch rectangle, with the long side closest to you. Sprinkle half of the mozzarella and Parmesan cheeses over the dough leaving an empty 1-inch border from the edge farthest away from you. Spoon the roasted vegetables over the cheese, sprinkle the olives over everything and top with the remaining cheese.
4. Start rolling the stromboli away from you and toward the empty border. Make sure the filling stays tightly tucked inside the roll. Finally, tuck the ends of the dough in and pinch the seam shut. Place the seam side down and shape the stromboli into a U-shape to fit into the air fryer basket. Cut 4 small slits with the tip of a sharp knife evenly in the top of the dough, lightly brush the stromboli with a little oil and sprinkle with some dried oregano.
5. Preheat the air fryer to 360°F.
6. Spray or brush the air fryer basket with oil and transfer the U-shaped stromboli to the air fryer basket. Air-fry for 15 minutes, flipping the stromboli over after the first 10 minutes. (Use a plate to invert the Stromboli out of the air fryer basket and then slide it back into the basket off the plate.)
7. To remove, carefully flip the stromboli over onto a cutting board. Let it rest for a couple of minutes before serving. Cut it into 2-inch slices and serve with pizza or marinara sauce.

Quinoa Burgers With Feta Cheese And Dill

Servings: 6   Cooking Time: 10 Minutes

Ingredients:

- 1 cup quinoa (red, white or multi-colored)
- 1½ cups water
- 1 teaspoon salt
- freshly ground black pepper
- 1½ cups rolled oats
- 3 eggs, lightly beaten
- ¼ cup minced white onion
- ½ cup crumbled feta cheese
- ¼ cup chopped fresh dill
- salt and freshly ground black pepper
- vegetable or canola oil, in a spray bottle
- whole-wheat hamburger buns (or gluten-free hamburger buns*)
- arugula
- tomato, sliced
- red onion, sliced
- mayonnaise

Directions:

1. Make the quinoa: Rinse the quinoa in cold water in a saucepan, swirling it with your hand until any dry husks rise to the surface. Drain the quinoa as well as you can and then put the saucepan on the stovetop to dry and toast the quinoa. Turn the heat to medium-high and shake the pan regularly until you see the quinoa moving easily and can hear the seeds moving in the pan, indicating that they are dry. Add the water, salt and pepper. Bring the liquid to a boil and then reduce the heat to low or medium-low. You should see just a few bubbles, not a boil. Cover with a lid, leaving it askew and simmer for 20 minutes. Turn the heat off and fluff the quinoa with a fork. If there's any liquid left in the bottom of the pot, place it back on the burner for another 3 minutes or so. Spread the cooked quinoa out on a sheet pan to cool.

2. Combine the room temperature quinoa in a large bowl with the oats, eggs, onion, cheese and dill. Season with salt and pepper and mix well (remember that feta cheese is salty). Shape the mixture into 6 patties with flat sides (so they fit more easily into the air fryer). Add a little water or a few more rolled oats if necessary to get the mixture to be the right consistency to make patties.

3. Preheat the air-fryer to 400°F.

4. Spray both sides of the patties generously with oil and transfer them to the air fryer basket in one layer (you will probably have to cook these burgers in batches, depending on the size of your air fryer). Air-fry each batch at 400°F for 10 minutes, flipping the burgers over halfway through the cooking time.

5. Build your burger on the whole-wheat hamburger buns with arugula, tomato, red onion and mayonnaise.

Corn And Pepper Jack Chile Rellenos With Roasted Tomato Sauce

Servings: 3   Cooking Time: 30 Minutes

Ingredients:

- 3 Poblano peppers
- 1 cup all-purpose flour*
- salt and freshly ground black pepper
- 2 eggs, lightly beaten
- 1 cup plain breadcrumbs*
- olive oil, in a spray bottle
- Sauce
- 2 cups cherry tomatoes
- 1 Jalapeño pepper, halved and seeded
- 1 clove garlic

- ¼ red onion, broken into large pieces
- 1 tablespoon olive oil
- salt, to taste
- 2 tablespoons chopped fresh cilantro
- Filling
- olive oil
- ¼ red onion, finely chopped
- 1 teaspoon minced garlic
- 1 cup corn kernels, fresh or frozen
- 2 cups grated pepper jack cheese

Directions:

1. Start by roasting the peppers. Preheat the air fryer to 400°F. Place the peppers into the air fryer basket and air-fry at 400°F for 10 minutes, turning them over halfway through the cooking time. Remove the peppers from the basket and cover loosely with foil.

2. While the peppers are cooling, make the roasted tomato sauce. Place all sauce Ingredients except for the cilantro into the air fryer basket and air-fry at 400°F for 10 minutes, shaking the basket once or twice. When the sauce Ingredients have finished air-frying, transfer everything to a blender or food processor and blend or process to a smooth sauce, adding a little warm water to get the desired consistency. Season to taste with salt, add the cilantro and set aside.

3. While the sauce Ingredients are cooking in the air fryer, make the filling. Heat a skillet on the stovetop over medium heat. Add the olive oil and sauté the red onion and garlic for 4 to 5 minutes. Transfer the onion and garlic to a bowl, stir in the corn and cheese, and set aside.

4. Set up a dredging station with three shallow dishes. Place the flour, seasoned with salt and pepper, in the first shallow dish. Place the eggs in the second dish, and fill the third shallow dish with the breadcrumbs. When the peppers have cooled, carefully slice into one side of the pepper to create an opening. Pull the seeds out of the peppers and peel away the skins, trying not to tear the pepper. Fill each pepper with some of the corn and cheese filling and close the pepper up again by folding one side of the opening over the other. Carefully roll each pepper in the seasoned flour, then into the egg and finally into the breadcrumbs to coat on all sides, trying not to let the pepper fall open. Spray the peppers on all sides with a little olive oil.

5. Air-fry two peppers at a time at 350°F for 6 minutes. Turn the peppers over and air-fry for another 4 minutes. Serve the peppers warm on a bed of the roasted tomato sauce.

Asparagus, Mushroom And Cheese Soufflés

Servings: 3	Cooking Time: 21 Minutes

Ingredients:

- butter
- grated Parmesan cheese
- 3 button mushrooms, thinly sliced
- 8 spears asparagus, sliced ½-inch long
- 1 teaspoon olive oil
- 1 tablespoon butter
- 4½ teaspoons flour

- pinch paprika
- pinch ground nutmeg
- salt and freshly ground black pepper
- ½ cup milk
- ½ cup grated Gruyère cheese or other Swiss cheese (about 2 ounces)
- 2 eggs, separated

Directions:

1. Butter three 6-ounce ramekins and dust with grated Parmesan cheese. (Butter the ramekins and then coat the butter with Parmesan by shaking it around in the ramekin and dumping out any excess.)

2. Preheat the air fryer to 400°F.

3. Toss the mushrooms and asparagus in a bowl with the olive oil. Transfer the vegetables to the air fryer and air-fry for 7 minutes, shaking the basket once or twice to redistribute the Ingredients while they cook.

4. While the vegetables are cooking, make the soufflé base. Melt the butter in a saucepan on the stovetop over medium heat. Add the flour, stir and cook for a minute or two. Add the paprika, nutmeg, salt and pepper. Whisk in the milk and bring the mixture to a simmer to thicken. Remove the pan from the heat and add the cheese, stirring to melt. Let the mixture cool for just a few minutes and then whisk the egg yolks in, one at a time. Stir in the cooked mushrooms and asparagus. Let this soufflé base cool.

5. In a separate bowl, whisk the egg whites to soft peak stage (the point at which the whites can almost stand up on the end of your whisk). Fold the whipped egg whites into the soufflé base, adding a little at a time.

6. Preheat the air fryer to 330°F.

7. Transfer the batter carefully to the buttered ramekins, leaving about ½-inch at the top. Place the ramekins into the air fryer basket and air-fry for 14 minutes. The soufflés should have risen nicely and be brown on top. Serve immediately.

Arancini With Marinara

Servings: 6

Cooking Time: 15 Minutes

Ingredients:

- ➢ 2 cups cooked rice
- ➢ 1 cup grated Parmesan cheese
- ➢ 1 egg, whisked
- ➢ ¼ teaspoon dried thyme
- ➢ ½ teaspoon dried oregano
- ➢ ½ teaspoon dried basil
- ➢ ½ teaspoon dried parsley
- ➢ 1 teaspoon salt
- ➢ ¼ teaspoon paprika
- ➢ 1 cup breadcrumbs
- ➢ 4 ounces mozzarella, cut into 24 cubes
- ➢ 2 cups marinara sauce

Directions:

1. In a large bowl, mix together the rice, Parmesan cheese, and egg.
2. In another bowl, mix together the thyme, oregano, basil, parsley, salt, paprika, and breadcrumbs.
3. Form 24 rice balls with the rice mixture. Use your thumb to make an indentation in the center and stuff 1 cube of mozzarella in the center of the rice; close the ball around the cheese.
4. Roll the rice balls in the seasoned breadcrumbs until all are coated.
5. Preheat the air fryer to 400°F.
6. Place the rice balls in the air fryer basket and coat with cooking spray. Cook for 8 minutes, shake the basket, and cook another 7 minutes.
7. Heat the marinara sauce in a saucepan until warm. Serve sauce as a dip for arancini.

Curried Potato, Cauliflower And Pea Turnovers

Servings: 4   Cooking Time: 40 Minutes

Ingredients:

- Dough:
- 2 cups all-purpose flour
- ½ teaspoon baking powder
- 1 teaspoon salt
- freshly ground black pepper
- ¼ teaspoon dried thyme
- ¼ cup canola oil
- ½ to ⅔ cup water
- Turnover Filling:
- 1 tablespoon canola or vegetable oil
- 1 onion, finely chopped
- 1 clove garlic, minced
- 1 tablespoon grated fresh ginger
- ½ teaspoon cumin seeds
- ½ teaspoon fennel seeds
- 1 teaspoon curry powder
- 2 russet potatoes, diced
- 2 cups cauliflower florets
- ½ cup frozen peas
- 2 tablespoons chopped fresh cilantro
- salt and freshly ground black pepper
- 2 tablespoons butter, melted
- mango chutney, for serving

Directions:

1. Start by making the dough. Combine the flour, baking powder, salt, pepper and dried thyme in a mixing bowl or the bowl of a stand mixer. Drizzle in the canola oil and pinch it together with your fingers to turn the flour into a crumby mixture. Stir in the water (enough to bring the dough together). Knead the dough for 5 minutes or so until it is smooth. Add a little more water or flour as needed. Let the dough rest while you make the turnover filling.

2. Preheat a large skillet on the stovetop over medium-high heat. Add the oil and sauté the onion until it starts to become tender – about 4 minutes. Add the garlic and ginger and continue to cook for another minute. Add the dried spices and toss everything to coat. Add the potatoes and cauliflower to the skillet and pour in 1½ cups of water. Simmer everything together for 20 to 25 minutes, or until the potatoes are soft and most of the water has evaporated. If the water has evaporated and the vegetables still need more time, just add a little water and continue to simmer until everything is tender. Stir well, crushing the potatoes and cauliflower a little as you do so. Stir in the peas and cilantro, season to taste with salt and freshly ground black pepper and set aside to cool.

3. Divide the dough into 4 balls. Roll the dough balls out into ¼-inch thick circles. Divide the cooled potato filling between the dough circles, placing a mound of the filling on one side of each piece of dough, leaving an empty border around the edge of the dough. Brush the edges of the dough with a little water and fold one edge of circle over the filling to meet the other edge of the circle, creating a half

moon. Pinch the edges together with your fingers and then press the edge with the tines of a fork to decorate and seal.

4. Preheat the air fryer to 380°F.

5. Spray or brush the air fryer basket with oil. Brush the turnovers with the melted butter and place 2 turnovers into the air fryer basket. Air-fry for 15 minutes. Flip the turnovers over and air-fry for another 5 minutes. Repeat with the remaining 2 turnovers.

6. These will be very hot when they come out of the air fryer. Let them cool for at least 20 minutes before serving warm with mango chutney.

Parmesan Portobello Mushroom Caps

Servings: 2	Cooking Time: 14 Minutes

Ingredients:

- ¼ cup flour*
- 1 egg, lightly beaten
- 1 cup seasoned breadcrumbs*
- 2 large portobello mushroom caps, stems and gills removed

- olive oil, in a spray bottle
- ½ cup tomato sauce
- ¾ cup grated mozzarella cheese
- 1 tablespoon grated Parmesan cheese
- 1 tablespoon chopped fresh basil or parsley

Directions:

1. Set up a dredging station with three shallow dishes. Place the flour in the first shallow dish, egg in the second dish and breadcrumbs in the last dish. Dredge the mushrooms in flour, then dip them into the egg and finally press them into the breadcrumbs to coat on all sides. Spray both sides of the coated mushrooms with olive oil.

2. Preheat the air fryer to 400°F.

3. Air-fry the mushrooms at 400°F for 10 minutes, turning them over halfway through the cooking process.

4. Fill the underside of the mushrooms with the tomato sauce and then top the sauce with the mozzarella and Parmesan cheeses. Reset the air fryer temperature to 350°F and air-fry for an additional 4 minutes, until the cheese has melted and is slightly browned.

5. Serve the mushrooms with pasta tossed with tomato sauce and garnish with some chopped fresh basil or parsley.

Sandwiches And Burgers Recipes

Chili Cheese Dogs

Servings: 3

Cooking Time: 12 Minutes

Ingredients:

- ¾ pound Lean ground beef
- 1½ tablespoons Chile powder
- 1 cup plus 2 tablespoons Jarred sofrito
- 3 Hot dogs (gluten-free, if a concern)
- 3 Hot dog buns (gluten-free, if a concern), split open lengthwise
- 3 tablespoons Finely chopped scallion
- 9 tablespoons (a little more than 2 ounces) Shredded Cheddar cheese

Directions:

1. Crumble the ground beef into a medium or large saucepan set over medium heat. Brown well, stirring often to break up the clumps. Add the chile powder and cook for 30 seconds, stirring the whole time. Stir in the sofrito and bring to a simmer. Reduce the heat to low and simmer, stirring occasionally, for 5 minutes. Keep warm.

2. Preheat the air fryer to 400°F.

3. When the machine is at temperature, put the hot dogs in the basket and air-fry undisturbed for 10 minutes, or until the hot dogs are bubbling and blistered, even a little crisp.

4. Use kitchen tongs to put the hot dogs in the buns. Top each with a ½ cup of the ground beef mixture, 1 tablespoon of the minced scallion, and 3 tablespoons of the cheese. (The scallion should go under the cheese so it superheats and wilts a bit.) Set the filled hot dog buns in the basket and air-fry undisturbed for 2 minutes, or until the cheese has melted.

5. Remove the basket from the machine. Cool the chili cheese dogs in the basket for 5 minutes before serving.

Perfect Burgers

Servings: 3

Cooking Time: 13 Minutes

Ingredients:

➢ 1 pound 2 ounces 90% lean ground beef

➢ 1½ tablespoons Worcestershire sauce (gluten-free, if a concern)

➢ ½ teaspoon Ground black pepper

➢ 3 Hamburger buns (gluten-free if a concern), split open

Directions:

1. Preheat the air fryer to 375°F .

2. Gently mix the ground beef, Worcestershire sauce, and pepper in a bowl until well combined but preserving as much of the meat's fibers as possible. Divide this mixture into two 5-inch patties for the small batch, three 5-inch patties for the medium, or four 5-inch patties for the large. Make a thumbprint indentation in the center of each patty, about halfway through the meat.

3. Set the patties in the basket in one layer with some space between them. Air-fry undisturbed for 10 minutes, or until an instant-read meat thermometer inserted into the center of a burger registers 160°F (a medium-well burger). You may need to add 2 minutes cooking time if the air fryer is at 360°F.

4. Use a nonstick-safe spatula, and perhaps a flatware fork for balance, to transfer the burgers to a cutting board. Set the buns cut side down in the basket in one layer (working in batches as necessary) and air-fry undisturbed for 1 minute, to toast a bit and warm up. Serve the burgers in the warm buns.

Thanksgiving Turkey Sandwiches

Servings: 3   Cooking Time: 10 Minutes

Ingredients:

- 1½ cups Herb-seasoned stuffing mix (not cornbread-style; gluten-free, if a concern)
- 1 Large egg white(s)
- 2 tablespoons Water
- 3 5- to 6-ounce turkey breast cutlets
- Vegetable oil spray
- 4½ tablespoons Purchased cranberry sauce, preferably whole berry
- ⅛ teaspoon Ground cinnamon
- ⅛ teaspoon Ground dried ginger
- 4½ tablespoons Regular, low-fat, or fat-free mayonnaise (gluten-free, if a concern)
- 6 tablespoons Shredded Brussels sprouts
- 3 Kaiser rolls (gluten-free, if a concern), split open

Directions:

1. Preheat the air fryer to 375°F .

2. Put the stuffing mix in a heavy zip-closed bag, seal it, lay it flat on your counter, and roll a rolling pin over the bag to crush the stuffing mix to the consistency of rough sand. (Or you can pulse the stuffing mix to the desired consistency in a food processor.)

3. Set up and fill two shallow soup plates or small pie plates on your counter: one for the egg white(s), whisked with the water until foamy; and one for the ground stuffing mix.

4. Dip a cutlet in the egg white mixture, coating both sides and letting any excess egg white slip back into the rest. Set the cutlet in the ground stuffing mix and coat it evenly on both sides, pressing gently to coat well on both sides. Lightly coat the cutlet on both sides with vegetable oil spray, set it aside, and continue dipping and coating the remaining cutlets in the same way.

5. Set the cutlets in the basket and air-fry undisturbed for 10 minutes, or until crisp and brown. Use kitchen tongs to transfer the cutlets to a wire rack to cool for a few minutes.

6. Meanwhile, stir the cranberry sauce with the cinnamon and ginger in a small bowl. Mix the shredded Brussels sprouts and mayonnaise in a second bowl until the vegetable is evenly coated.

7. Build the sandwiches by spreading about 1½ tablespoons of the cranberry mixture on the cut side of the bottom half of each roll. Set a cutlet on top, then spread about 3 tablespoons of the Brussels sprouts mixture evenly over the cutlet. Set the other half of the roll on top and serve warm.

Thai-style Pork Sliders

Servings: 4

Cooking Time: 15 Minutes

Ingredients:

➢ 11 ounces Ground pork

➢ 2½ tablespoons Very thinly sliced scallions, white and green parts

➢ 4 teaspoons Minced peeled fresh ginger

➢ 2½ teaspoons Fish sauce (gluten-free, if a concern)

➢ 2 teaspoons Thai curry paste (see the headnote; gluten-free, if a concern)

➢ 2 teaspoons Light brown sugar

➢ ¾ teaspoon Ground black pepper

➢ 4 Slider buns (gluten-free, if a concern)

Directions:

1. Preheat the air fryer to 375°F .

2. Gently mix the pork, scallions, ginger, fish sauce, curry paste, brown sugar, and black pepper in a bowl until well combined. With clean, wet hands, form about ⅓ cup of the pork mixture into a slider about 2½ inches in diameter. Repeat until you use up all the meat—3 sliders for the small batch, 4 for the medium, and 6 for the large. (Keep wetting your hands to help the patties adhere.)

3. When the machine is at temperature, set the sliders in the basket in one layer. Air-fry undisturbed for 14 minutes, or until the sliders are golden brown and caramelized at their edges and an instant-read meat thermometer inserted into the center of a slider registers 160°F.

4. Use a nonstick-safe spatula, and perhaps a flatware fork for balance, to transfer the sliders to a cutting board. Set the buns cut side down in the basket in one layer (working in batches as necessary) and air-fry undisturbed for 1 minute, to toast a bit and warm up. Serve the sliders warm in the buns.

White Bean Veggie Burgers

Servings: 3

Cooking Time: 13 Minutes

Ingredients:

- 1⅓ cups Drained and rinsed canned white beans
- 3 tablespoons Rolled oats (not quick-cooking or steel-cut; gluten-free, if a concern)
- 3 tablespoons Chopped walnuts
- 2 teaspoons Olive oil
- 2 teaspoons Lemon juice
- 1½ teaspoons Dijon mustard (gluten-free, if a concern)
- ¾ teaspoon Dried sage leaves
- ¼ teaspoon Table salt
- Olive oil spray
- 3 Whole-wheat buns or gluten-free whole-grain buns (if a concern), split open

Directions:

1. Preheat the air fryer to 400°F.

2. Place the beans, oats, walnuts, oil, lemon juice, mustard, sage, and salt in a food processor. Cover and process to make a coarse paste that will hold its shape, about like wet sugar-cookie dough, stopping the machine to scrape down the inside of the canister at least once.

3. Scrape down and remove the blade. With clean and wet hands, form the bean paste into two 4-inch patties for the small batch, three 4-inch patties for the medium, or four 4-inch patties for the large batch. Generously coat the patties on both sides with olive oil spray.

4. Set them in the basket with some space between them and air-fry undisturbed for 12 minutes, or until lightly brown and crisp at the edges. The tops of the burgers will feel firm to the touch.

5. Use a nonstick-safe spatula, and perhaps a flatware fork for balance, to transfer the burgers to a cutting board. Set the buns cut side down in the basket in one layer (working in batches as necessary) and air-fry undisturbed for 1 minute, to toast a bit and warm up. Serve the burgers warm in the buns.

Dijon Thyme Burgers

Servings: 3   Cooking Time: 18 Minutes

Ingredients:

- 1 pound lean ground beef
- ⅓ cup panko breadcrumbs
- ¼ cup finely chopped onion
- 3 tablespoons Dijon mustard
- 1 tablespoon chopped fresh thyme
- 4 teaspoons Worcestershire sauce
- 1 teaspoon salt

- freshly ground black pepper
- Topping (optional):
- 2 tablespoons Dijon mustard
- 1 tablespoon dark brown sugar
- 1 teaspoon Worcestershire sauce
- 4 ounces sliced Swiss cheese, optional

Directions:

1. Combine all the burger ingredients together in a large bowl and mix well. Divide the meat into 4 equal portions and then form the burgers, being careful not to over-handle the meat. One good way to do this is to throw the meat back and forth from one hand to another, packing the meat each time you catch it. Flatten the balls into patties, making an indentation in the center of each patty with your thumb (this will help it stay flat as it cooks) and flattening the sides of the burgers so that they will fit nicely into the air fryer basket.

2. Preheat the air fryer to 370°F.

3. If you don't have room for all four burgers, air-fry two or three burgers at a time for 8 minutes. Flip the burgers over and air-fry for another 6 minutes.

4. While the burgers are cooking combine the Dijon mustard, dark brown sugar, and Worcestershire sauce in a small bowl and mix well. This optional topping to the burgers really adds a boost of flavor at the end. Spread the Dijon topping evenly on each burger. If you cooked the burgers in batches, return the first batch to the cooker at this time – it's ok to place the fourth burger on top of the others in the center of the basket. Air-fry the burgers for another 3 minutes.

5. Finally, if desired, top each burger with a slice of Swiss cheese. Lower the air fryer temperature to 330°F and air-fry for another minute to melt the cheese. Serve the burgers on toasted brioche buns, dressed the way you like them.

Inside Out Cheeseburgers

Servings: 2

Cooking Time: 20 Minutes

Ingredients:

- ¾ pound lean ground beef
- 3 tablespoons minced onion
- 4 teaspoons ketchup
- 2 teaspoons yellow mustard
- salt and freshly ground black pepper
- 4 slices of Cheddar cheese, broken into smaller pieces
- 8 hamburger dill pickle chips

Directions:

1. Combine the ground beef, minced onion, ketchup, mustard, salt and pepper in a large bowl. Mix well to thoroughly combine the ingredients. Divide the meat into four equal portions.

2. To make the stuffed burgers, flatten each portion of meat into a thin patty. Place 4 pickle chips and half of the cheese onto the center of two of the patties, leaving a rim around the edge of the patty exposed. Place the remaining two patties on top of the first and press the meat together firmly, sealing the edges tightly. With the burgers on a flat surface, press the sides of the burger with the palm of your hand to create a straight edge. This will help keep the stuffing inside the burger while it cooks.

3. Preheat the air fryer to 370°F.

4. Place the burgers inside the air fryer basket and air-fry for 20 minutes, flipping the burgers over halfway through the cooking time.

5. Serve the cheeseburgers on buns with lettuce and tomato.

Inside-out Cheeseburgers

Servings: 3

Cooking Time: 9-11 Minutes

Ingredients:

- ➢ 1 pound 2 ounces 90% lean ground beef
- ➢ ¾ teaspoon Dried oregano
- ➢ ¾ teaspoon Table salt
- ➢ ¾ teaspoon Ground black pepper
- ➢ ¼ teaspoon Garlic powder
- ➢ 6 tablespoons (about 1½ ounces) Shredded Cheddar, Swiss, or other semi-firm cheese, or a purchased blend of shredded cheeses
- ➢ 3 Hamburger buns (gluten-free, if a concern), split open

Directions:

1. Preheat the air fryer to 375°F .
2. Gently mix the ground beef, oregano, salt, pepper, and garlic powder in a bowl until well combined without turning the mixture to mush. Form it into two 6-inch patties for the small batch, three for the medium, or four for the large.
3. Place 2 tablespoons of the shredded cheese in the center of each patty. With clean hands, fold the sides of the patty up to cover the cheese, then pick it up and roll it gently into a ball to seal the cheese inside. Gently press it back into a 5-inch burger without letting any cheese squish out. Continue filling and preparing more burgers, as needed.
4. Place the burgers in the basket in one layer and air-fry undisturbed for 8 minutes for medium or 10 minutes for well-done. (An instant-read meat thermometer won't work for these burgers because it will hit the mostly melted cheese inside and offer a hotter temperature than the surrounding meat.)
5. Use a nonstick-safe spatula, and perhaps a flatware fork for balance, to transfer the burgers to a cutting board. Set the buns cut side down in the basket in one layer (working in batches as necessary) and air-fry undisturbed for 1 minute, to toast a bit and warm up. Cool the burgers a few minutes more, then serve them warm in the buns.

Crunchy Falafel Balls

Servings: 8

Cooking Time: 16 Minutes

Ingredients:

- ➢ 2½ cups Drained and rinsed canned chickpeas
- ➢ ¼ cup Olive oil
- ➢ 3 tablespoons All-purpose flour
- ➢ 1½ teaspoons Dried oregano
- ➢ 1½ teaspoons Dried sage leaves
- ➢ 1½ teaspoons Dried thyme
- ➢ ¾ teaspoon Table salt
- ➢ Olive oil spray

Directions:

1. Preheat the air fryer to 400°F.

2. Place the chickpeas, olive oil, flour, oregano, sage, thyme, and salt in a food processor. Cover and process into a paste, stopping the machine at least once to scrape down the inside of the canister.

3. Scrape down and remove the blade. Using clean, wet hands, form 2 tablespoons of the paste into a ball, then continue making 9 more balls for a small batch, 15 more for a medium one, and 19 more for a large batch. Generously coat the balls in olive oil spray.

4. Set the balls in the basket in one layer with a little space between them and air-fry undisturbed for 16 minutes, or until well browned and crisp.

5. Dump the contents of the basket onto a wire rack. Cool for 5 minutes before serving.

Provolone Stuffed Meatballs

Servings: 4

Cooking Time: 12 Minutes

Ingredients:

- 1 tablespoon olive oil
- 1 small onion, very finely chopped
- 1 to 2 cloves garlic, minced
- ¾ pound ground beef
- ¾ pound ground pork
- ¾ cup breadcrumbs
- ¼ cup grated Parmesan cheese
- ¼ cup finely chopped fresh parsley (or 1 tablespoon dried parsley)
- ½ teaspoon dried oregano
- 1½ teaspoons salt
- freshly ground black pepper
- 2 eggs, lightly beaten
- 5 ounces sharp or aged provolone cheese, cut into 1-inch cubes

Directions:

1. Preheat a skillet over medium-high heat. Add the oil and cook the onion and garlic until tender, but not browned.

2. Transfer the onion and garlic to a large bowl and add the beef, pork, breadcrumbs, Parmesan cheese, parsley, oregano, salt, pepper and eggs. Mix well until all the ingredients are combined. Divide the mixture into 12 evenly sized balls. Make one meatball at a time, by pressing a hole in the meatball mixture with your finger and pushing a piece of provolone cheese into the hole. Mold the meat back into a ball, enclosing the cheese.

3. Preheat the air fryer to 380°F.

4. Working in two batches, transfer six of the meatballs to the air fryer basket and air-fry for 12 minutes, shaking the basket and turning the meatballs a couple of times during the cooking process. Repeat with the remaining six meatballs. You can pop the first batch of meatballs into the air fryer for the last two minutes of cooking to re-heat them. Serve warm.

Mexican Cheeseburgers

Servings: 4

Cooking Time: 22 Minutes

Ingredients:

- 1¼ pounds ground beef
- ¼ cup finely chopped onion
- ½ cup crushed yellow corn tortilla chips
- 1 (1.25-ounce) packet taco seasoning
- ¼ cup canned diced green chilies
- 1 egg, lightly beaten
- 4 ounces pepper jack cheese, grated
- 4 (12-inch) flour tortillas
- shredded lettuce, sour cream, guacamole, salsa (for topping)

Directions:

1. Combine the ground beef, minced onion, crushed tortilla chips, taco seasoning, green chilies, and egg in a large bowl. Mix thoroughly until combined – your hands are good tools for this. Divide the meat into four equal portions and shape each portion into an oval-shaped burger.

2. Preheat the air fryer to 370°F.

3. Air-fry the burgers for 18 minutes, turning them over halfway through the cooking time. Divide the cheese between the burgers, lower fryer to 340°F and air-fry for an additional 4 minutes to melt the cheese. (This will give you a burger that is medium-well. If you prefer your cheeseburger medium-rare, shorten the cooking time to about 15 minutes and then add the cheese and proceed with the recipe.)

4. While the burgers are cooking, warm the tortillas wrapped in aluminum foil in a 350°F oven, or in a skillet with a little oil over medium-high heat for a couple of minutes. Keep the tortillas warm until the burgers are ready.

5. To assemble the burgers, spread sour cream over three quarters of the tortillas and top each with some shredded lettuce and salsa. Place the Mexican cheeseburgers on the lettuce and top with guacamole. Fold the tortillas around the burger, starting with the bottom and then folding the sides in over the top. (A little sour cream can help hold the seam of the tortilla together.) Serve immediately.

Best-ever Roast Beef Sandwiches

Servings: 6

Cooking Time: 30-50 Minutes

Ingredients:

- 2½ teaspoons Olive oil
- 1½ teaspoons Dried oregano
- 1½ teaspoons Dried thyme
- 1½ teaspoons Onion powder
- 1½ teaspoons Table salt
- 1½ teaspoons Ground black pepper
- 3 pounds Beef eye of round
- 6 Round soft rolls, such as Kaiser rolls or hamburger buns (gluten-free, if a concern), split open lengthwise
- ¾ cup Regular, low-fat, or fat-free mayonnaise (gluten-free, if a concern)
- 6 Romaine lettuce leaves, rinsed
- 6 Round tomato slices (¼ inch thick)

Directions:

1. Preheat the air fryer to 350°F .

2. Mix the oil, oregano, thyme, onion powder, salt, and pepper in a small bowl. Spread this mixture all over the eye of round.

3. When the machine is at temperature, set the beef in the basket and air-fry for 30 to 50 minutes (the range depends on the size of the cut), turning the meat twice, until an instant-read meat thermometer inserted into the thickest piece of the meat registers 130°F for rare, 140°F for medium, or 150°F for well-done.

4. Use kitchen tongs to transfer the beef to a cutting board. Cool for 10 minutes. If serving now, carve into ⅛-inch-thick slices. Spread each roll with 2 tablespoons mayonnaise and divide the beef slices between the rolls. Top with a lettuce leaf and a tomato slice and serve. Or set the beef in a container, cover, and refrigerate for up to 3 days to make cold roast beef sandwiches anytime.

Lamb Burgers

Servings: 3

Cooking Time: 17 Minutes

Ingredients:

- ➤ 1 pound 2 ounces Ground lamb
- ➤ 3 tablespoons Crumbled feta
- ➤ 1 teaspoon Minced garlic
- ➤ 1 teaspoon Tomato paste
- ➤ ¾ teaspoon Ground coriander
- ➤ ¾ teaspoon Ground dried ginger
- ➤ Up to ⅛ teaspoon Cayenne
- ➤ Up to a ⅛ teaspoon Table salt (optional)
- ➤ 3 Kaiser rolls or hamburger buns (gluten-free, if a concern), split open

Directions:

1. Preheat the air fryer to 375°F .

2. Gently mix the ground lamb, feta, garlic, tomato paste, coriander, ginger, cayenne, and salt (if using) in a bowl until well combined, trying to keep the bits of cheese intact. Form this mixture into two 5-inch patties for the small batch, three 5-inch patties for the medium, or four 5-inch patties for the large.

3. Set the patties in the basket in one layer and air-fry undisturbed for 16 minutes, or until an instant-read meat thermometer inserted into one burger registers 160°F. (The cheese is not an issue with the temperature probe in this recipe as it was for the Inside-Out Cheeseburgers, because the feta is so well mixed into the ground meat.)

4. Use a nonstick-safe spatula, and perhaps a flatware fork for balance, to transfer the burgers to a cutting board. Set the buns cut side down in the basket in one layer (working in batches as necessary) and air-fry undisturbed for 1 minute, to toast a bit and warm up. Serve the burgers warm in the buns.

Fish And Seafood Recipes

Stuffed Shrimp

Servings: 4   Cooking Time: 12 Minutes Per Batch

Ingredients:

- 16 tail-on shrimp, peeled and deveined (last tail section intact)
- ¾ cup crushed panko breadcrumbs
- oil for misting or cooking spray
- Stuffing
- 2 6-ounce cans lump crabmeat
- 2 tablespoons chopped shallots
- 2 tablespoons chopped green onions
- 2 tablespoons chopped celery
- 2 tablespoons chopped green bell pepper
- ½ cup crushed saltine crackers
- 1 teaspoon Old Bay Seasoning
- 1 teaspoon garlic powder
- ¼ teaspoon ground thyme
- 2 teaspoons dried parsley flakes
- 2 teaspoons fresh lemon juice
- 2 teaspoons Worcestershire sauce
- 1 egg, beaten

Directions:

1. Rinse shrimp. Remove tail section (shell) from 4 shrimp, discard, and chop the meat finely.

2. To prepare the remaining 12 shrimp, cut a deep slit down the back side so that the meat lies open flat. Do not cut all the way through.

3. Preheat air fryer to 360°F.

4. Place chopped shrimp in a large bowl with all of the stuffing ingredients and stir to combine.

5. Divide stuffing into 12 portions, about 2 tablespoons each.

6. Place one stuffing portion onto the back of each shrimp and form into a ball or oblong shape. Press firmly so that stuffing sticks together and adheres to shrimp.

7. Gently roll each stuffed shrimp in panko crumbs and mist with oil or cooking spray.

8. Place 6 shrimp in air fryer basket and cook at 360°F for 10minutes. Mist with oil or spray and cook 2 minutes longer or until stuffing cooks through inside and is crispy outside.

9. Repeat step 8 to cook remaining shrimp.

Fish Tacos With Jalapeño-lime Sauce

Servings: 4   Cooking Time: 7 Minutes

Ingredients:

- Fish Tacos
- 1 pound fish fillets
- ¼ teaspoon cumin
- ¼ teaspoon coriander
- ⅛ teaspoon ground red pepper
- 1 tablespoon lime zest
- ¼ teaspoon smoked paprika
- 1 teaspoon oil
- cooking spray
- 6–8 corn or flour tortillas (6-inch size)

- Jalapeño-Lime Sauce
- ½ cup sour cream
- 1 tablespoon lime juice
- ¼ teaspoon grated lime zest
- ½ teaspoon minced jalapeño (flesh only)
- ¼ teaspoon cumin
- Napa Cabbage Garnish
- 1 cup shredded Napa cabbage
- ¼ cup slivered red or green bell pepper
- ¼ cup slivered onion

Directions:

1. Slice the fish fillets into strips approximately ½-inch thick.

2. Put the strips into a sealable plastic bag along with the cumin, coriander, red pepper, lime zest, smoked paprika, and oil. Massage seasonings into the fish until evenly distributed.

3. Spray air fryer basket with nonstick cooking spray and place seasoned fish inside.

4. Cook at 390°F for approximately 5minutes. Shake basket to distribute fish. Cook an additional 2 minutes, until fish flakes easily.

5. While the fish is cooking, prepare the Jalapeño-Lime Sauce by mixing the sour cream, lime juice, lime zest, jalapeño, and cumin together to make a smooth sauce. Set aside.

6. Mix the cabbage, bell pepper, and onion together and set aside.

7. To warm refrigerated tortillas, wrap in damp paper towels and microwave for 30 to 60 seconds.

8. To serve, spoon some of fish into a warm tortilla. Add one or two tablespoons Napa Cabbage Garnish and drizzle with Jalapeño-Lime Sauce.

Fish And "chips"

Servings: 2

Cooking Time: 10 Minutes

Ingredients:

- ½ cup flour
- ½ teaspoon paprika
- ¼ teaspoon ground white pepper (or freshly ground black pepper)
- 1 egg
- ¼ cup mayonnaise
- 2 cups salt & vinegar kettle cooked potato chips, coarsely crushed
- 12 ounces cod
- tartar sauce
- lemon wedges

Directions:

1. Set up a dredging station. Combine the flour, paprika and pepper in a shallow dish. Combine the egg and mayonnaise in a second shallow dish. Place the crushed potato chips in a third shallow dish.

2. Cut the cod into 6 pieces. Dredge each piece of fish in the flour, then dip it into the egg mixture and then place it into the crushed potato chips. Make sure all sides of the fish are covered and pat the chips gently onto the fish so they stick well.

3. Preheat the air fryer to 370°F.

4. Place the coated fish fillets into the air fry basket. (It is ok if a couple of pieces slightly overlap or rest on top of other fillets in order to fit everything in the basket.)

5. Air-fry for 10 minutes, gently turning the fish over halfway through the cooking time.

6. Transfer the fish to a platter and serve with tartar sauce and lemon wedges.

Lobster Tails With Lemon Garlic Butter

Servings: 2

Cooking Time: 5 Minutes

Ingredients:

➢ 4 ounces unsalted butter

➢ 1 tablespoon finely chopped lemon zest

➢ 1 clove garlic, thinly sliced

➢ 2 (6-ounce) lobster tails

➢ salt and freshly ground black pepper

➢ ½ cup white wine

➢ ½ lemon, sliced

➢ vegetable oil

Directions:

1. Start by making the lemon garlic butter. Combine the butter, lemon zest and garlic in a small saucepan. Melt and simmer the butter on the stovetop over the lowest possible heat while you prepare the lobster tails.

2. Prepare the lobster tails by cutting down the middle of the top of the shell. Crack the bottom shell by squeezing the sides of the lobster together so that you can access the lobster meat inside. Pull the lobster tail up out of the shell, but leave it attached at the base of the tail. Lay the lobster meat on top of the shell and season with salt and freshly ground black pepper. Pour a little of the lemon garlic butter on top of the lobster meat and transfer the lobster to the refrigerator so that the butter solidifies a little.

3. Pour the white wine into the air fryer drawer and add the lemon slices. Preheat the air fryer to 400°F for 5 minutes.

4. Transfer the lobster tails to the air fryer basket. Air-fry at 370° for 5 minutes, brushing more butter on halfway through cooking. (Add a minute or two if your lobster tail is more than 6-ounces.) Remove and serve with more butter for dipping or drizzling.

Bacon-wrapped Scallops

Servings: 4

Cooking Time: 8 Minutes

Ingredients:

➤ 16 large scallops

➤ 8 bacon strips

➤ ½ teaspoon black pepper

➤ ¼ teaspoon smoked paprika

Directions:

1. Pat the scallops dry with a paper towel. Slice each of the bacon strips in half. Wrap 1 bacon strip around 1 scallop and secure with a toothpick. Repeat with the remaining scallops. Season the scallops with pepper and paprika.

2. Preheat the air fryer to 350°F.

3. Place the bacon-wrapped scallops in the air fryer basket and cook for 4 minutes, shake the basket, cook another 3 minutes, shake the basket, and cook another 1 to 3 to minutes. When the bacon is crispy, the scallops should be cooked through and slightly firm, but not rubbery. Serve immediately.

Lemon-dill Salmon Burgers

Servings: 4

Cooking Time: 8 Minutes

Ingredients:

- ➢ 2 (6-ounce) fillets of salmon, finely chopped by hand or in a food processor
- ➢ 1 cup fine breadcrumbs
- ➢ 1 teaspoon freshly grated lemon zest
- ➢ 2 tablespoons chopped fresh dill weed
- ➢ 1 teaspoon salt
- ➢ freshly ground black pepper
- ➢ 2 eggs, lightly beaten
- ➢ 4 brioche or hamburger buns
- ➢ lettuce, tomato, red onion, avocado, mayonnaise or mustard, to serve

Directions:

1. Preheat the air fryer to 400°F.

2. Combine all the ingredients in a bowl. Mix together well and divide into four balls. Flatten the balls into patties, making an indentation in the center of each patty with your thumb (this will help the burger stay flat as it cooks) and flattening the sides of the burgers so that they fit nicely into the air fryer basket.

3. Transfer the burgers to the air fryer basket and air-fry for 4 minutes. Flip the burgers over and air-fry for another 3 to 4 minutes, until nicely browned and firm to the touch.

4. Serve on soft brioche buns with your choice of topping – lettuce, tomato, red onion, avocado, mayonnaise or mustard.

Horseradish-crusted Salmon Fillets

Servings: 3

Cooking Time: 8 Minutes

Ingredients:

➤ ½ cup Fresh bread crumbs (see the headnote)

➤ 4 tablespoons (¼ cup/½ stick) Butter, melted and cooled

➤ ¼ cup Jarred prepared white horseradish

➤ Vegetable oil spray

➤ 4 6-ounce skin-on salmon fillets (for more information, see here)

Directions:

1. Preheat the air fryer to 400°F.

2. Mix the bread crumbs, butter, and horseradish in a bowl until well combined.

3. Take the basket out of the machine. Generously spray the skin side of each fillet. Pick them up one by one with a nonstick-safe spatula and set them in the basket skin side down with as much air space between them as possible. Divide the bread-crumb mixture between the fillets, coating the top of each fillet with an even layer. Generously coat the bread-crumb mixture with vegetable oil spray.

4. Return the basket to the machine and air-fry undisturbed for 8 minutes, or until the topping has lightly browned and the fish is firm but not hard.

5. Use a nonstick-safe spatula to transfer the salmon fillets to serving plates. Cool for 5 minutes before serving. Because of the butter in the topping, it will stay very hot for quite a while. Take care, especially if you're serving these fillets to children.

Buttery Lobster Tails

Servings:4

Cooking Time: 6 Minutes

Ingredients:

- ➢ 4 6- to 8-ounce shell-on raw lobster tails
- ➢ 2 tablespoons Butter, melted and cooled
- ➢ 1 teaspoon Lemon juice
- ➢ ½ teaspoon Finely grated lemon zest
- ➢ ½ teaspoon Garlic powder
- ➢ ½ teaspoon Table salt
- ➢ ½ teaspoon Ground black pepper

Directions:

1. Preheat the air fryer to 375°F .

2. To give the tails that restaurant look, you need to butterfly the meat. To do so, place a tail on a cutting board so that the shell is convex. Use kitchen shears to cut a line down the middle of the shell from the larger end to the smaller, cutting only the shell and not the meat below, and stopping before the back fins. Pry open the shell, leaving it intact. Use your clean fingers to separate the meat from the shell's sides and bottom, keeping it attached to the shell at the back near the fins. Pull the meat up and out of the shell through the cut line, laying the meat on top of the shell and closing the shell (as well as you can) under the meat. Make two equidistant cuts down the meat from the larger end to near the smaller end, each about ¼ inch deep, for the classic restaurant look on the plate. Repeat this procedure with the remaining tail(s).

3. Stir the butter, lemon juice, zest, garlic powder, salt, and pepper in a small bowl until well combined. Brush this mixture over the lobster meat set atop the shells.

4. When the machine is at temperature, place the tails shell side down in the basket with as much air space between them as possible. Air-fry undisturbed for 6 minutes, or until the lobster meat has pink streaks over it and is firm.

5. Use kitchen tongs to transfer the tails to a wire rack. Cool for only a minute or two before serving.

Pecan-orange Crusted Striped Bass

Servings: 2   Cooking Time: 9 Minutes

Ingredients:

- flour, for dredging*
- 2 egg whites, lightly beaten
- 1 cup pecans, chopped
- 1 teaspoon finely chopped orange zest, plus more for garnish
- ½ teaspoon salt
- 2 (6-ounce) fillets striped bass

- salt and freshly ground black pepper
- vegetable or olive oil, in a spray bottle
- Orange Cream Sauce (Optional)
- ½ cup fresh orange juice
- ¼ cup heavy cream
- 1 sprig fresh thyme

Directions:

1. Set up a dredging station with three shallow dishes. Place the flour in one shallow dish. Place the beaten egg whites in a second shallow dish. Finally, combine the chopped pecans, orange zest and salt in a third shallow dish.

2. Coat the fish fillets one at a time. First season with salt and freshly ground black pepper. Then coat each fillet in flour. Shake off any excess flour and then dip the fish into the egg white. Let the excess egg drip off and then immediately press the fish into the pecan-orange mixture. Set the crusted fish fillets aside.

3. Preheat the air fryer to 400°F.

4. Spray the crusted fish with oil and then transfer the fillets to the air fryer basket. Air-fry for 9 minutes at 400°F, flipping the fish over halfway through the cooking time. The nuts on top should be nice and toasty and the fish should feel firm to the touch.

5. If you'd like to make a sauce to go with the fish while it cooks, combine the freshly squeezed orange juice, heavy cream and sprig of thyme in a small saucepan. Simmer on the stovetop for 5 minutes and then set aside.

6. Remove the fish from the air fryer and serve over a bed of salad, like the one below. Then add a sprinkling of orange zest and a spoonful of the orange cream sauce over the top if desired.

Blackened Red Snapper

Servings: 4

Cooking Time: 8 Minutes

Ingredients:

- 1½ teaspoons black pepper
- ¼ teaspoon thyme
- ¼ teaspoon garlic powder
- ⅛ teaspoon cayenne pepper
- 1 teaspoon olive oil
- 4 4-ounce red snapper fillet portions, skin on
- 4 thin slices lemon
- cooking spray

Directions:

1. Mix the spices and oil together to make a paste. Rub into both sides of the fish.
2. Spray air fryer basket with nonstick cooking spray and lay snapper steaks in basket, skin-side down.
3. Place a lemon slice on each piece of fish.
4. Cook at 390°F for 8 minutes. The fish will not flake when done, but it should be white through the center.

Flounder Fillets

Servings: 4

Cooking Time: 8 Minutes

Ingredients:

➢ 1 egg white

➢ 1 tablespoon water

➢ 1 cup panko breadcrumbs

➢ 2 tablespoons extra-light virgin olive oil

➢ 4 4-ounce flounder fillets

➢ salt and pepper

➢ oil for misting or cooking spray

Directions:

1. Preheat air fryer to 390°F.

2. Beat together egg white and water in shallow dish.

3. In another shallow dish, mix panko crumbs and oil until well combined and crumbly (best done by hand).

4. Season flounder fillets with salt and pepper to taste. Dip each fillet into egg mixture and then roll in panko crumbs, pressing in crumbs so that fish is nicely coated.

5. Spray air fryer basket with nonstick cooking spray and add fillets. Cook at 390°F for 3minutes.

6. Spray fish fillets but do not turn. Cook 5 minutes longer or until golden brown and crispy. Using a spatula, carefully remove fish from basket and serve.